MY TRIP DOWN THE
PINK CARPET

MY TRIP DOWN THE
PINK CARPET

LESLIE JORDAN

SIMON SPOTLIGHT ENTERTAINMENT
New York

Simon Spotlight Entertainment
A Division of Simon & Schuster, Inc.
1230 Avenue of the Americas
New York, NY 10020

First Simon Spotlight Entertainment trade paperback edition June 2009

SIMON SPOTLIGHT ENTERTAINMENT and colophon are trademarks
of Simon & Schuster, Inc.

For information about special discounts for bulk purchases,
please contact Simon & Schuster Special Sales at 1-866-506-1949
or business@simonandschuster.com.

The Simon & Schuster Speakers Bureau can bring authors to
your live event. For more information or to book an event contact the
Simon & Schuster Speakers Bureau at 1-866-248-3049 or visit our
website at www.simonspeakers.com.

Designed by Gabe Levine

Manufactured in the United States of America

1 3 5 7 9 10 8 6 4 2

The Library of Congress has cataloged the hardcover edition as follows:
Jordan, Leslie.
My trip down the pink carpet / Leslie Jordan.
p.   cm.
1. Jordan, Leslie.   2. Actors—United States—Biography.
3. Gay actors—United States—Biography.   I. Title.
PN2287.J67 A3 2008
792.02'8092—dc22
[B]
2008006901

ISBN 978-1-4169-5555-9
ISBN 978-1-4391-5348-2 (pbk)

*This book is dedicated to three of my favorite
Southern ladies: my roommate of twenty years,
Miss Carla Holland, who watched it unfold
from afar but never once bought into the insanity;
Miss Dale Davis, who always gave me laughter,
courage, and hope; and my sweet mother,
Peggy Ann Jordan, who bore it all with
a great amount of fortitude.*

If I live to be one hundred and five years old, I will never understand this deep-seated need you have to air your dirty laundry! Why can't you just whisper it to a therapist?

Peggy Ann Jordan, my witty and
wonderful mother

Contents

Introduction

I stood backstage at the 2006 Emmy Awards in a blind panic.

The week before, at the Creative Arts Emmys, I had been awarded Outstanding Guest Actor in a Comedy Series for my work on *Will & Grace*. Because of that win, I had been invited to become a presenter at the Emmys. I was to present awards for outstanding comedy writing and outstanding comedy directing with my copresenter, Miss Cloris Leachman.

But the question at hand was, where in the world was Cloris?

I had been told by the stage manager that she had suffered a "wardrobe malfunction." Wasn't that the term used for that unfortunate incident involving Janet Jackson? My God, had her *breast* popped out? The woman was eighty years old! No, I was told, someone had stepped on the train of her dress and ripped it all the way up the side.

Why, I wondered, would anyone in her right mind wear a dress with a train to this cattle stampede? But that seemed to be "the look" of the 2006 Emmys. I had yelled hello to Debra Messing as we were herded into the Shrine Auditorium and she, too, was bent over, thrashing through waves and waves of white net, trying to sort out her train. Apparently she had also been stepped on by some oblivious Emmy attendee.

"Is Miss Leachman going to make it in time?" I nervously inquired. "I do not want to go out there alone!"

Too bad I'm eight years sober, I thought. I remembered some "advice" that Mr. Pat Buttram, the wonderful character actor who played Mr. Haney on *Green Acres,* had given me years earlier, when we were doing a live radio drama from the Gene Autry Museum. As the two of us stood off-stage, ready to make our entrance, Mr. Buttram pulled a silver flask from his back pocket, held the flask aloft, and offered me a swig.

"No . . . no thank you, Mr. Buttram," I stammered.

He stared at me in disbelief. "You go out there *alone*?"

But now I was without a flask and could not avail myself of a swig of courage even if I had wanted to. Besides, it was not worth losing eight years of sobriety to Miss Leachman's wardrobe malfunction.

"Oh, thank God, here she comes!" I heard the stage manager cry.

I spotted Miss Leachman, parading regally toward us like the Queen of Sheba, with a coterie of wardrobe assistants knee walking while frantically sewing and stapling her dress together.

The stage manager yelled above the backstage din, "And in five . . . four . . . three . . . two . . ."

Cloris grabbed up the mended part of her dress and took my hand in hers, and we swept onstage to thunderous applause—in honor of her eighth prime-time Emmy win. She was now the most decorated actress in Emmy history, surpassing Mary Tyler Moore by one. I looked out over that enormous audience filled with the biggest and brightest Hollywood stars and stood rooted to the spot.

Oh my gosh.

My introduction to the magic of Hollywood had taken place in a darkened motion picture theatre in Chattanooga, Tennessee, in 1959. My mother took me to see *Darby O'Gill and the Little People*. I was barely four years old, but I stared wide-eyed at the big screen and did not move or make a peep for an hour and a half. On the ride home, I stood in the back seat and boldly began to belt out the theme song at the top of my little lungs: "Oh, she is my dear and darlin' one. Her eyes are sparklin' full of fun . . ."

I remembered most of the words. And what I did not remember, I made up.

In 1982, I stepped off a Greyhound bus at the corner of Vine Street and De Longpre Avenue in downtown Hollywood. I had twelve hundred dollars sewn into my underpants. I had a tiny suitcase. And I had dreams. I had dreams as big as the California sky! You see, back where I grew up in East Tennessee, there were lots of hills and lots of foliage, but when I stepped off that bus, all I saw was sky.

Bless my sweet, simple heart!

I had no idea what I was up against. Bear in mind that 1982 was years before *The Ellen De Generes Show*. It was years before *Queer Eye for the Straight Guy, Queer as Folk,* and *Will & Grace*. Foremost in my mind as I stepped off that bus was: *It might not be a good idea to let anyone know that I am a homosexual.* I decided I was going to make a real effort to "butch it up" and hide any signs that I was a Big Homo.

The funny thing is, I am, without a doubt, the gayest man I know. I fell right out of the womb and landed smack dab in my mama's high heels. With all due disrespect to the Christian Right, ain't none of that "choice" shit here! But I was so riddled with internal homophobia, so consumed with doubt, shame, and self-hatred, that I felt the need to try and pull it off. My devout Southern Baptist upbringing had left me with beliefs that were indelible, at least at that time in my life.

. . .

Cloris pulled me from my reverie. "You know, dear, I've won eight of these, but one never forgets the first one."

"Oh, Miss Leachman," I gushed, "I take mine everywhere with me! I even sleep with it! It's the only woman I've ever slept with."

Huge laughter.

Sitting in the first few rows were Warren Beatty and Annette Bening, Geena Davis, Kyra Sedgwick and Kevin Bacon, Megan Mullally, Julia Louis-Dreyfus, Heidi Klum and Seal, John Lithgow, Jeffrey Tambor, Stockard Channing, Blythe Danner, Calista Flockhart, Harrison Ford, Bob Newhart, Ray Liotta, James Woods, Candice Bergen, William Shatner. The list went on and on. Not to mention the big guns from England, Jeremy Irons and Helen Mirren.

Oh my gosh.

So how did this self-conscious young man, who stepped off the bus in 1982 riddled with shame and inner homophobia, become the silver-haired, confident, openly gay man who stood before a jury of his peers in 2006 to present one of the highest awards possible—and throw out the line "It's the only woman I've ever slept with" without hesitation, without one iota of self-doubt, and certainly without any shame?

Well, this is my trip down the pink carpet.

These are my stories.

These are my songs.

American Dreams

FAIRLY EARLY in my career, I was hired to do a two-episode arc of a situation comedy called *American Dreamer*. *American Dreamer* starred Robert Urich and the delightful Carol Kane. I cannot for the life of me remember what the show was about. It was terribly high-concept, with Robert Urich delivering long monologues in the dark, wearing a black turtleneck.

What a crush I had on Robert Urich! It was a

sophomoric crush going all the way back to the days when he was the hot young tennis pro on *Soap*. What a dreamboat! I realize that using the term "dreamboat" is a bit unseemly for a man my age. But I'll admit it right here and now: I am a high school cheerleader stuck in an old man's body!

To this day, I still write in my diary nightly. Most of the entries deal with my current crush. You would not believe how I gush and carry on. (Well, maybe you would.) I am an infatuation junkie. Like most gay men my age, I have no earthly idea how to love in a healthy and blessed manner. I only know how to obsess. Lord knows, I'm real good at that. And trust me, I ain't alone here.

But who can fault us? When all those red-blooded heterosexual males were slowly learning the fundamentals of flirting and dating in junior high, finding healthy ways to deal with all that teenage-love shit, where were we? Where were the queers? We were hiding out within the confines of our Big Secret, that's where. We were locked in the recesses of our own minds, forlornly sitting in the back row of homeroom, creating fantasies in our heads.

Oh, the crushes I had at Dalewood Junior High School in the mid-1960s! All unrequited, all angst-ridden, and all completely made up.

One week it would be the quarterback of our football team. I'd sit and stare at the back of his head for hours and hours, memorizing the look of his perfect ears, and how his hair just barely brushed the collar of his button-down oxford cloth shirt. I was forced to endure the torture of watching a chirpy cheerleader flirt outrageously with *my* quarterback. I silently plotted her murder as I seethed with jealousy. Who did Little Miss Perky Breasts think she was? I would go home, put on Tammy Wynette, and cry my eyes out.

"Stand by your man! Give him two arms to cling to. . . ."

I'd wail and wail. And then I decided I'd show that quarterback a thing or two. Yes, ma'am, I'd turn the tables on him. I dropped him like a hot potato and moved on to the cutest boy in the whole school. What a steamy tumultuous affair that was! Oh yes, he and I had some real good times. If I recall correctly, I got pregnant. I spent the entire summer carrying his love child. This time I sat in my bedroom, still all alone, singing along with Diana Ross in her big-afro period.

"Love child . . . Never quite as good. Afraid, ashamed, misunderstood . . ."

But I digress.

On *American Dreamer* I played Ralph Short, the shortest member of the FBI. Ralph Short was a real man's man. He was the kind of man that makes up for his lack of physical stature by strutting around like a bandy rooster. I was a little concerned about "pulling this one off." To make matters worse, the first day of the shoot, I was approached by the director, who looked me right in the eye.

"I want to be really up-front with you," he said. "You were not my choice for this part. I am somewhat familiar with your work and I think you are a wonderful actor. But you carry a certain kind of baggage that I do not think works for this particular character."

I carry a certain kind of baggage?

No shit.

Why don't you just come out and say it? I remember thinking. *Why tiptoe around the truth? I am a big fag! I am a screaming sissy, a poof, a nancy boy, a silly, prancing, simpering nellie fairy. I am a little too light in the loafers, a little too fey. Right? Let's just lay our cards on the table, shall we?*

And then he said, "But not to worry, I am going to work with you."

Work with me? How? Teach me in ten easy lessons? If this wasn't a recipe for disaster, I didn't know what was. I'd spent a lifetime trying to walk and talk like a man.

The first time I heard my voice recorded, I was mortified. I was twelve years old and coming out of that tinny little tape recorder was not me, but Butterfly McQueen, the actress who played Prissy in *Gone with the Wind*. The shame of it all! I sounded just like a *girl*. I had "the accent," and I ain't talking about my Southern accent. It's the gay thing. I open my mouth and the whole world knows. It is plain and simple.

When I was in the fourth grade, I came home from school with a small wooden box I had been given by a speech therapist. In the box was a tongue depressor, a mirror, and instructions on how to rid oneself of "the sibilant *s*." What is "the sibilant *s*?" you may ask. Well, it's a dead giveaway for a fag, that's what. It's not really a lisp, it's more of a hissing sound. I sat with that heinous box for hours with the tongue depressor in my mouth, my eyes on the mirror, and the instructions unfolded in front of me.

"Sssally sssellsss ssseashellsss by the ssseashore. Sssally sssellsss ssseashellssss by the ssseashore."

Hopeless.

When I was in the ninth grade, the telephone number of a pervert was passed around school. Some girls having a slumber party had stumbled upon this degenerate while making prank phone calls. Boy, my ears perked right up. I secretly memorized the phone number, then rushed home and dialed him up. As he breathed heavily and masturbated loudly, he asked me all sorts of inappropriate questions, like "What color are your panties?"

I boldly told him I didn't wear any! Not even to cheerleader practice! *That* really got him going.

"Does the hair on your little pussy match the hair on your head?" he whispered in a raspy voice.

Shocking!

But I rolled with the punches. I giggled and told him coyly that they were both flame red and real bushy. This was before the "Brazilian" became the look—back when several stray hairs playing peek-a-boo out of a girl's bathing suit bottom could send a pimply-faced boy into a masturbatory frenzy. Even *Playboy* magazine in that era was demure with pubic hair. The best you could hope for was a glimpse of a muff behind a see-though scarf.

My conversations with the pervert turned me into a dirty little slut. I spent weeks on the phone getting filthier and filthier. It all came to a head when I dared him to meet me in the booths near the refreshment counter of the drugstore across the street from my school. What was going through my head? Had I lost my marbles? I told him in no uncertain terms that he could not approach me or speak to me but that I would sit in a booth across from him, lift my cheerleader skirt, and give him a good shot of "my bushy red beaver" when nobody was looking.

When the day arrived, I hid out in a back booth, sipped on a cherry Coke, and waited with bated breath. I suppose behind my flagrant behavior was a desperate need to put a face to that obscene voice. I thought I was going to faint as I watched the front door and nervously twirled the ice in my Coke.

I was expecting someone who looked like the janitor at my school. He wore his Levi's blue jeans so tight you could see the outline of his big tally-whacker, had his wallet on a chain, and spent a lot of time in the boys' room in front of the mirror combing his hair à la Elvis. I'd lock myself in a toilet stall and peep out the crack in the door just to watch him. Sometimes he would pose obscenely, grabbing his privates and whispering nasty things to the mirror. "You want a little of this?"

Or perhaps my pervert would look like a hot, young Robert Blake in *In Cold Blood*. I had once brazenly taken a city bus to the movie theatre one Saturday morning all by myself to see a double feature: *In Cold Blood* plus *The Boston Strangler,* starring an equally hot, brooding Tony Curtis.

But I sat for hours in the drugstore, and nobody showed up. I drank so many cherry Cokes I nearly floated out. I guess my pervert thought it was a sting operation. I'm sure it's probably for the best. There is no telling what sort of mischief I would have gotten into had he actually arrived.

Not that he would have come over to me. To have pulled off such a charade, I must have sounded exactly like a girl. And still, to this day, over the telephone, especially when I'm angry, I get, "Ma'am. Ma'am, you need to calm down."

"I'm *not* a ma'am! I am a *sssir*. I am a gay sssir, but nonetheless, a sssir."

What in the world to do about the problem of my overtly sissy nature became the set joke on *American Dreamer*. The whole cast and crew began to pitch in. Everyone wanted to help me become more of a man's man. Everything was up for grabs. Nothing was sacred.

I would be standing casually, chatting with Carol Kane, when out of the blue some electrician would lean in and whisper, "You need to take a wider stance."

I would be on the phone, bitching to my agent, when all of a sudden I would hear someone say, "Put your voice in a lower register."

I would be sitting with my legs crossed, which I have done since kindergarten, when I figured out that it was more comfortable, and hear, "I wouldn't sit like that if I were you."

Somewhere along the way during the two-week shoot it got a little ugly. I'm not sure why. Perhaps the director had gotten notes from the Powers That Be. Or maybe the director did not feel that I was giving it my all. He probably had no idea what he was up against.

It all came to a head when the director got so frustrated he pulled me aside and said, "This is not the road tour of *Tru*. Are you going to work with me or not?"

It took me a few minutes to ascertain what he meant.

Oh dear.

Tru was a play about Truman Capote. Long before I realized my true nature or even what that meant, I innately knew that Truman Capote and I were the same. I was both repulsed and deeply fascinated as I watched him on *The Tonight Show*, lisping to Johnny Carson. But I would eventually have to leave the room when he was on TV, my feelings were so strong. I really thought I would vomit. I felt the same way when Paul Lynde was the "center square" of *Hollywood Squares*. It all seemed really shameful.

This is not the road tour of Tru. *Are you going to work with me or not?*

I was devastated. It really started to affect me. I would be at home all alone watching TV and catch myself curled up like a cat. I would immediately unfurl myself and find a way to sit that more befit the manly man everyone was trying to make out of me.

The night we shot *American Dreamer* in front of a studio audience, I was a mess. In one scene, I had to stand offstage with a bullhorn and deliver my lines. When the moment arrived, I assumed a manly pose and hollered, "Tom! Tom! Open up! It's Ralph Short with the FBI! Open up or we're coming in!"

Huge laughter.

Oh dear. That line was not supposed to be funny.

Situation comedies are taped without the director on the floor. Instead, he sits up in a booth calling the camera shots. When the director needs to speak to the actors, he does so over a loudspeaker, and essentially (to me, anyway) sounds like the voice of God. The director stopped the action and called down to me.

"Leslie? Who is out there?"

I put my voice in a lower register and yelled, "Ralph Short with the FBI!"

"*Who* is out there?"

I took an even wider stance and lowered my voice as much as possible. "Ralph Short with the FBI!"

"Who is out there?"

I screamed, "RALPH SHORT WITH THE FBI!"

"Could have sworn it was Charles Nelson Reilly!"

Huge laughter.

You might think that I detest this director to this day. But you had to be there. It was all in fun. It really was. It is not his fault that this particular issue was my hot button. I do not believe there is a homophobic bone in his body. He did not mean to be cruel, he just wanted to get a good performance out of me. He wanted to see me do something that I had never done before. He'd told me that he was going to work with me—and he did.

When I saw the episode, I was floored. When you work in situation comedies as much as I have, you tend to acquire a little bag of tricks. I am the proud founder and the guiding light of the Leslie Jordan School of Mugging. But the director was having none of that, and as a result, my performance was top-notch. You did not see Leslie Jordan at all. And, more important for the character, you did not see "gay" at all. In a strange way, I was very proud of that.

I had pulled it off!

Many years later, I was called in to read for a new movie called *The Mighty Ducks*. The character I was to audition for was a hockey coach.

A hockey coach?

I thought, *I'm not sure I can pull* that *off*. I started to turn down the audition but my agent told me the director had specifically asked for me.

Yep, the same director was at the helm. There was much hemming and hawing in my mind. Did I want to go through another butch-Leslie-up session?

When I got to the audition, the director told the people in the room, "This is one of the funniest men you will ever meet." God bless him. I almost started crying.

Needless to say, I did not get the part.

Good Southern Stock

My mother always said, "Stop making a spectacle of yourself," something that I have obviously made a career out of.

John Waters, *Spectacle*

MY MOTHER was a bashful champagne blonde who always smelled of White Shoulders perfume.

On special occasions she would dab on a little Shalimar. She always conducted herself with a great amount of class. She was never one to succumb to fads, and she wore her hair in a modified bouffant. It was very glamorous—Jackie Kennedy with just a little touch of the Supremes— and it had an amazing flip to the side that she sprayed with a cloud of Aqua Net.

I was so proud that she was my mom. Her name was Peggy Ann and to me she was the most beautiful woman in the world. I thought she was a fairy princess. When the other mothers showed up for the Parent Teacher Association meetings in frumpy housedresses, my mother was always perfectly turned out. Until I was almost out of grammar school, she wore white gloves when she left the house. She looked like a fashion model from the pages of a magazine.

I also adored my mother's mother. Her name was Mary Lucille Griffin. My mother was the baby of eight children, and I suppose that's why she was so spoiled. When she was growing up, what she couldn't get from her mother and father, she got from her brothers and sisters. Mary Lucille had raised all of her children on a plumber's salary and was known for feeding the neighborhood kids as well. She was the best cook in all of Hamilton County. It was more than just a rumor that Grandmother Griffin's red velvet cake could make a Baptist get up and dance.

When poor Mary Lucille was practically on her deathbed, my mother decided that it would be a shame for all those wonderful recipes to go with her. My grandmother, like most Southern cooks of her era, cooked without any written recipes. It was a pinch of this and a little of that. I know, because out of all the grandkids I was the only one who took a real interest in the way she cooked. I would follow beside her in the kitchen as she whirled about in her flour-covered apron, making her delicious tea cakes.

My mother decided that it was up to us to get all those recipes on paper. So off we went to Grandmother's house with my Big Chief tablet in hand. Mary Lucille was trying to nap, but my mother was not to be deterred. She gently poked her and whispered, "Mama? About your biscuits?"

"What?" Mary Lucille asked, without opening her eyes.

"Leslie Allen and I are going to write down the recipe for your biscuits."

"Oh Lord, Peggy Ann, do we have to do it

now? I wanted to rest a little before my stories come on."

Mary Lucille's "stories" were her beloved soap operas. She watched them every afternoon without fail. One time we went to her house and the television was off. She was in bed during her stories and got us all worried. Granddaddy Griffin explained that Lynette had been framed and was in jail. She'd just found out she was pregnant with Hawk's baby. Poor Lynette was going to have the baby behind bars. It had upset my grandmother so much she had to take to the bed. We thought he was talking about some of our trashy relatives, but it turned out Lynette was the heroine of Mary Lucille's soap opera.

My mother persisted. "It's now or never. How much flour, Mama?"

Mary Lucille thought for a while, then opened her eyes. "Well, let me see. Enough to make a nest."

"Make a nest? That doesn't make sense."

"I know what she means," I piped in. "You pour enough flour in the bowl to pat it out and then it looks like a nest."

"Well, all right. Write that down. How much shortening, Mama?"

As I scribbled in my Big Chief tablet, Mary Lucille held up two shaky fingers, then promptly rolled over and went right back to sleep.

My mother sat there looking befuddled.

"I know what she means," I said again. "She means you take your two fingers and scrape them into the Crisco. And that's how much shortening you plop in the bowl."

"Well, Lord help us all, we can't write that down."

So our little project came to a disappointing end.

I get most of my sense of humor from my Granddaddy Griffin. Homer Howard Griffin was a stitch until the day they put him in his grave. Even in his nineties he had the nurses at the hospital eating out of his hand because of his amazing sense of humor. He liked to talk a little dirty, much to the delight of us grandkids. And Lord knows, with eight children there were a lot of grandkids.

One time, he was cutting up at the dinner table, and my favorite aunt Dot said, "Daddy, when you talk like that in front of the children it makes my skin crawl."

Granddaddy Griffin cocked his head inquisitively and said, "Well, Dot, what does your *heinie* smell like when it crawls past your *face*?"

All of us kids just hollered.

When Grandaddy died, I was performing with a melodrama troupe in Bakersfield, California. It was my first acting job after college and I was in heaven. I was making $165 a week! My mother called and tearfully told me, "Your biggest fan passed on this morning."

And he was. He really was my biggest fan. Even toward the end, when he was crazy as a bedbug and did not recognize anyone else, I would walk in the room and he'd say, "Leslie Allen, can you help spring me out of here?"

I had other fans from the beginning. When I was little, I think both Peggy Ann and Mary Lucille took one look at me and thought, *He's going to need some help!*

They circled the wagons, as only true Southern women can do, and created a secret garden where it was okay for little boys to play with dolls. How sweet is that? It was also okay for little boys to read about Trixie Belden and Nancy Drew instead of those rambunctious Hardy Boys. And it was okay for little boys to make potholders and sew doll clothes. I was "artistic," and they encouraged me in that arena. But somehow, even at a young age, I knew it was best to not let Daddy into our little secret garden. So even though I was allowed to do what I wanted, I knew it was somehow shameful.

My daddy, Allen Bernard Jordan, was a man's man. He was as handsome as a movie star. Even though he stood a little less than five feet five, he was in possession of an easy kind of masculinity that both awes and terrifies me—and that I am extremely attracted to. I've been in therapy about *that* for years.

My daddy used to call me "son" as if he was in deep pain. He'd say, "Oh, son," and it would sound like "sohhhn."

One of my early ambitions was to be a go-go dancer. I used to sit and watch the dancers on a TV show called *Hullabaloo,* which was the MTV of my generation. I was transfixed as the dancers wildly cavorted on white platforms. I knew it took a lot of practice to achieve that level of expertise, so I pushed all the furniture in the living room out of the way and commandeered the coffee table. Once I had mastered "the Jerk," I moved on to the next level, which included "the Swim" and "the Hitchhiker." After several weeks of intense practice, I also had "the Batman" and "Mashed Potato" under my belt. By the time my repertoire included "the Dirty Dog," which involved a whole lot of hunching and some really intricate facial expressions, I was on my way.

My poor daddy would come home and his firstborn son would be feverishly go-go dancing on the coffee table to "Wipeout" by the Safaris.

"Daddy, watch me do the Pony!" I'd squeal as I hopped from foot to foot, jerking my head back and forth.

"Oh, *son*," he'd sigh.

My career hopes were dashed when I noticed that one of the boy dancers on *Hullabaloo* had bleached bangs. This was before even the Beach Boys had bleached bangs, and I thought that was the coolest thing I had ever seen. I talked my friend Charlie into helping me achieve my new look. We took hydrogen peroxide and combed it through my bangs, which promptly turned bright orange. When confronted by my daddy at the dinner table, I swore right over my Chef Boyardee ravioli that I didn't know what had happened. I just woke up that morning and there it was. Orange bangs. Can you believe it?

He did not believe it.

I got a good whipping for that. Not because I bleached my hair but because I lied. The whipping apparently did not do a lick of good, since when I was growing up I could lie with the greatest of ease. I have been in therapy about this, too.

Anyway, it was so disheartening. If I couldn't even get away with bleached bangs, how on earth was I ever, *ever* going to get away with high-heeled, pointy-toed Italian boots and skintight, striped pencil pants?

So I gave up my dream of becoming a go-go dancer and replaced it with dreams of becoming a majorette. My mother had been a majorette in high school (aren't they all in Tennessee?). I pulled out her baton one sweltering summer afternoon and begged her to show me a routine. I had always been fascinated with batons. My daddy had once taken me to a football game and tried patiently to explain all the ins and outs of football.

"Now, son, that is the offense and that is the defense."

I tugged on his sleeve and asked impatiently, "Daddy, when do the majorettes come out?"

"Oh, *son* . . ."

On that summer afternoon, Mother showed me a few of her best moves and that was all it took. I began to practice with a vengeance. I was in the front yard going to town with my baton when my daddy pulled up with his army buddies in tow.

"Daddy! Daddy! Watch me twirl!" I yelled in my high, squeaky voice.

"Oh, son," he lamented, pulling me aside, away from the pitying eyes of his buddies. "Why don't you twirl that little baton in the house?"

"Mama's afraid I'll break something!" I threw the baton over my head, did a big final twirl, and caught it in a pose. I wanted to show those big, butch army boys a thing or two.

"Son, I'll pay for whatever you break! Just please twirl in the house."

Now, don't get me wrong. My daddy was a good man. I adored my daddy. Everyone did. My daddy was a churchgoing man who lived his faith. He was a man with a code and he lived by that code. He was a deacon, a Sunday school teacher, and a pillar of the community. It was said that he "never met a stranger." My daddy was the kind of man who talked to people in the grocery store checkout lane. When all the car windows were rolled down in the summertime, he'd strike up conversations with other drivers at stoplights. My sisters and I would get down on the floorboard of the car because we were so embarrassed.

My daddy could walk into a room and light it up. And he was doing the best he could with "the light he had to see with," as my spiritual advisor once told me. It was the 1950s, and what was the greatest fear a man could have? That his son would turn out queer.

My daddy was killed in a plane crash when I was eleven years old. That is a terrible time for any boy to lose his daddy. He was so loved in the community that all the schools closed for his funeral and the church was packed to capacity with mourners.

But when my daddy died, I just knew to the very core of my being that he went to his grave a little ashamed to have a son like me. And at that age I didn't even know what "like me" meant. I just knew I was different.

I sometimes feel like I was born ashamed.

Playing the Part

For, look you, there is humor in all things, and the truest
philosophy is that which teaches us to find it and make
the most of it.

> Jack Point in *The Yeomen of the Guard*
> by Gilbert and Sullivan

THE AWFUL part about Hollywood is how people
in the industry try to pigeonhole you into a "type."
I was once described as a Danny DeVito type.

What? We're both short and we each have a penis. But that's about all I have in common with Danny DeVito.

I think one of the secrets to the little bit of success I have had in Hollywood is that I refused to change anything about myself. Not that I could if I tried. A long time ago, I decided that I would never be like Robert De Niro or Meryl Streep. I would never be the kind of actor who could disappear into the roles he or she played. And quite frankly, I have never been asked to play a character I felt was more interesting than me in real life.

So I just do the best Leslie Jordan I can. And I've done pretty well.

When I first arrived in Tinseltown, I met a casting director named Pamela Sparks. She was a really fun gal from Texas. Pam sat me down and gave me some advice.

"Honey," she said, "you are already so limited in what you can do because you have such a character look, with that elfin face, short stature, and those big ears. I think you really need to concentrate on losing your accent, especially in commercials. It regionalizes the product and advertising people don't want that."

The hilarious thing was that back then I thought I had actually *lost* my accent. My goodness gracious, I had a degree in theatre from the University of Tennessee at Chattanooga! I had taken all kinds of classes in speech and elocution.

But I went to work to rid myself of my Tennessee accent. I tried everything. I walked around with a pencil between my teeth. I bought a bunch of boring tapes from the Samuel French Bookstore. I decided the only way to truly get rid of my accent was to drop it entirely from my daily life—but I just wasn't willing to do that. I felt like such a fake. I am Southern to the bone. It's what I am. I felt like it was what set me apart from all the hundreds of other character actors that were getting off the bus daily.

So I set sail, accent and all.

Years later, Pam Sparks was casting a situation comedy starring Isabel Sanford, after her long run on *The Jeffersons*. It was called *Isabel's Honeymoon Hotel,* and one of the main characters was a security guard who kept shooting himself in the foot. They were looking for a Don Knotts type. I auditioned for everyone under the sun. Finally, I was standing outside Fred Silverman's office. (He was a TV god in those days.) Pam Sparks had her hand on the doorknob. I could tell by the way she was sweating that a lot was at stake with this audition.

"Now, listen, sweetie," she said. "Don't change a thing. Just do the same brilliant audition you've been doing."

Out of spite I said, "Well, Pam, you gave me some advice once that I've decided to take. So I've been working real hard and I've decided to do the audition without my Tennessee accent."

She turned pale and looked like she was going to faint. "Don't you fucking do this to me, Leslie."

"I was kidding! Honey, I was just kidding!"

She breathed a deep sigh of relief. "Well, standing outside Fred Silverman's office with our asses on the line is no time to kid. I have really talked you up. Now cut the shit, get in there, and be brilliant!"

The year I stepped off the bus in Hollywood—1982—was the year a wonderful character actor named Clara Peller hollered "Where's the beef?" and ushered in a whole new era in commercials. Character actors became the rage.

I worked up a storm. I was the Del Taco guy

and the PIP Printing guy. I was the elevator operator to Hamburger Hell (where people go who do not eat tacos) for Taco Bell. I was lost at sea dreaming about pancakes for Aunt Jemina Lite syrup. I was a hapless Christmas tree salesman, a busboy, a window washer, a dumb army private. But, alas, I was never the "hero" of the commercial. I was always the guy who mowed his lawn with the lawn mower that blew smoke, or drove his car with gas that "causes knocks." The hapless wonder! The clown! The loser! This did not do wonders for my self-esteem.

One of my first commercial agents was an old, cigar-chomping guy. My phone rang one day and he said, "Hey, kid, listen, I got a little something for you. They're looking for a spokesperson for the Selective Service."

I was a little taken aback. "Do you mean the organization that gets boys to join the army?"

"Yeah, you got a problem with that?"

I was hesitant. The spokesperson for the Selective Service? A little queer like me trying to convince young boys to join the army? Who was he kidding? But at that point in my career I was game for anything.

The Selective Service had decided to do a public service announcement putting the word out that all males were required to register at the post office within thirty days of their eighteenth birthday. In this particular television spot, a young man was seen lying in bed asleep on his eighteenth birthday. All of a sudden, his guardian angel pops up on the headboard and reminds him that today might be a good day to register with the Selective Service.

I was auditioning for the part of the guardian angel. When I got to the audition, I was handed a copy of the script. Actors at commercial auditions are usually not given much time to look over the words before the audition, so I quickly read through the script and almost fell over. It was filled with words that contained the dreaded sibilant s—which I was convinced would be a dead giveaway that I was queer.

It was terrifying.

"Hey, Ralph! Guesss what today isss? The SS-Selective SSServissse ssspecifically ssstatesss you mussst regissster at the possst offissse within thirty daysss of your eighteenth birthday. Why not do it today, Ralph?"

When I finished my audition all I got was a very terse thank you. I left the audition feeling very depressed, and very *gay*. But when I got home, the phone rang. It was my commercial agent.

I got the job!

I began to panic. I spent the next week holed up in my little Hollywood apartment practicing in front of a mirror. I knew it was imperative that I not come off as too gay. I tried lowering my voice. I tried sitting with my legs spread far apart, as if I was airing out my big gonads. I tried keeping my hands from fluttering in the air too much.

On the day we were to shoot the commercial, I walked on the set and everywhere I looked I saw enormous, masculine men in army suits. The troops had arrived! It was as if my daddy and all his buddies were there. It was like an acid flashback. The director called action and I jumped into my new "butch" mode and really tried to sell it.

"Cut!" The director walked over and gave me a puzzled look. "What happened to the flighty little angel that I hired? Did John Wayne eat him?"

Huge laughter.

I was so embarrassed. The director then asked me to please just do the part the way I did it in the audition. We did it over and over until he got what he wanted. That damn commercial ran for ten years. It haunted me. It was so hard for me to watch. Even though all my friends would compliment me on my performance, and tell me I was adorable, funny, and lovable, all I saw was a big sissy.

Another time, I was hired to do a series of Foster's beer commercials. The star of the commercial was Paul Hogan, before he became famous as "Crocodile" Dundee. I was supposed to sit at the bar drinking beer with Mr. Hogan as he waxed poetic about "shark wrestling" from Down Under. Hogan barely spoke to me, and when he did, I could not understand a word he said. On camera, he enunciated his words, but off camera, he didn't seem to be speaking English. He made me nervous. I thought any minute he might challenge me to a pissing contest or make me box a kangaroo.

I was sure he knew I was a queer and that's why he wasn't being very nice to me. Of course, back then I thought anyone who wasn't being nice to me knew I was a queer. (Now, I know Hogan could not *really* have been homophobic, as he eventually married Linda Kozlowski, his lovely costar in *"Crocodile" Dundee*. I knew Linda before that picture spiraled her to stardom, and she had many gay friends and a huge entourage of gay men who followed her around everywhere.)

There was something else that made me nervous. A good friend of mine from Australia told me that the rumor floating around Sydney was that Mr. Hogan had a twelve-inch penis. That is impossible! I went home and pulled out my ruler from elementary school. That's *huge*!

I remember years ago, sitting in a dirty-movie theatre watching the porn star John Holmes, who was supposed to have an enormous penis. His big thing was always flaccid. It was never fully erect. It just sort of hung off his skinny torso and flopped all over the place like a grotesque sausage. I was not impressed at all. He was just going through the motions. He would grunt and stuff his penis into whatever it had to be stuffed into and that was it. There was no passion, no fake groans, nothing. Then the bad 1970s porno music would start and there it was! Just a big slab of meat stuck in some cavernous, hairy, hippie vagina. What was the audience supposed to do then? Clap?

When I was sitting on the bar stool with Mr. Hogan, I couldn't get those nasty movies with John Holmes out of my head. I kept hearing that bad porno music. Every time I looked at Hogan I saw naughty pictures, which preyed upon my mind. I envisioned him trying to stuff something into something. It made me terribly tense and out of sorts.

And it did not help matters that the director kept fussing at me. He wanted a two-shot of us, but Hogan kept hogging the shot. I could have sworn he was elbowing me out of the way. I was certain at the time it was because I was a homo.

Finally, in desperation, the director took me aside and asked me what the problem was. I told him that Mr. Hogan was hogging the shot. He looked like he didn't believe me, so I told him to watch closely on the next take. Afterwards he came over and apologized, and said that a two-shot was imperative and I would just have to push my way into the picture. The cameras rolled again, and Hogan mumbled something about shark wrestling. I sat there in character and hung on his every word.

"*Shark wrestling?*" I asked, wide-eyed. This was my only line.

Then it was time for the two-shot. I was supposed to laugh uproariously and lean in to Mr. Hogan as if we were now best friends. Here goes! I threw back my head, laughing like a hyena, and then shoved my way right into the shot. I felt an elbow but that did not stop me. I was a man on a mission. I don't think Hogan was too happy with my brazen attempts to get into the picture, but such is life!

Years later, when Hogan became famous, I thought I had the inside track. I knew what made "Crocodile" Dundee so "cocky."

I was once hired to play a Ferengi on *Star Trek: The Next Generation*. Ferengi are extraterrestrial creatures with huge ears (where, supposedly, their erogenous zones are located). I was hired mainly because of my height. The job involved forty separate prosthetic pieces that were glued to my face, as well as fake teeth, contact lenses, and a very uncomfortable costume. I also had to be burned at the stake. I agreed to take the job because I needed the money.

I hold the distinction of working for the longest time in full prosthetics of any actor who has ever appeared in a *Star Trek* movie or television series. During the shoot, I was called into the makeup trailer at three o'clock in the morning and was not released until the following morning at two. Forget about overtime, I went into golden time. I was making a full day's salary every hour! At one point I was so tired I fell asleep, had a nightmare that I was drowning, and was woken up by a screaming makeup person—I had been clawing at my face, trying to pull off the rubber pieces.

But I soldiered on. The director called "Action!" and I paraded onto the spaceship and heroically delivered my first line.

"Cut!" yelled the director.

Huge laughter.

"This isn't Deep *South* Nine!" the director cackled. "Can you please bring that Ferengi a little north of the Mason–Dixon Line?"

It must have been hilarious to see this creature from outer space yelling with a thick Tennessee accent. It was like *Star Trek* meets *Hee Haw*.

The director was relentless. "Hey, Ferengi, the word 'feather' does not have four syllables, even in outer space. Lose the accent!"

The whole shoot was just torture. When I tried to lose my Tennessee accent, I would, for some unknown reason, lapse into a terrible Cockney impression.

"Hey, Ferengi! Now you sound like Eliza Doolittle on crack."

At one point, I locked myself in the bathroom and had a good cry. Thank God there weren't any of those people who gather at *Star Trek* conventions lurking about. Seeing a Ferengi boo-hooing on the toilet would be a Trekkie's dream come true.

I muddled through and they must have been pleased with the results because a week later, my agent called. "They want to bring your character back. And guess what? All your scenes will be with Whoopi Goldberg."

"I don't care if my scenes are with Jesus Christ," I said. "I don't want to be a Ferengi ever again. Do you hear me? I don't want to be on *Star Trek*."

From then on, whenever I was asked to lose my accent, I would respond by doing the audition over again—exactly the same way. The producers and the director would all just stare at me, not quite knowing what to say. I'm sure I lost a lot of jobs that way, but I didn't care. I was just being myself.

Monkey See, Monkey Do

Do you really want to hurt me?
Culture Club

I WAS once hired to play a monkey in a Japanese
sake commercial with Boy George. I was to lead
Boy George across the desert while he sat on
a white horse in full geisha drag, sipping sake.
There would also be a dancing pig and a big green
bird.

We were told these were very recognizable Japanese fairy-tale characters.

We were all hauled out to the middle of the Mojave Desert in California: Boy George, his entourage, the actor playing the dancing pig, the actor playing the big green bird, myself, and a Japanese film crew of forty people. The crew did not speak a word of English. We were put up in the town of Baker, which was tiny. The only restaurant sat right across the street from our seedy motel. It was called the Bun Boy. Boy George thought that was hilarious.

I had to be in the makeup chair at three o'clock in the morning to be ready to go when the cameras rolled at eight. I had to lie still with straws up my nose for hours and hours. It was excruciatingly uncomfortable. And I thought show business was going to be glamorous!

The makeup artist was Rick Baker, who has won trillions of Oscars for his movie makeup magic. I emerged from the makeup trailer looking like a punk monkey with a huge Patti LaBelle hairdo. I was also fitted with fake monkey teeth and gold-specked contact lenses. I was then strapped into a kimono with six-foot flags sticking straight up.

By the time I was ready to go, I was exhausted. I called my agent in tears, begging him to get me out of this unholy situation. The only food was sushi that had been sitting in the desert sun for hours. The Japanese must have stomachs of iron. I, however, do not.

Getting Boy George to emerge from his trailer was such an ordeal. He's amazingly quick and clever but a tad mean-spirited. I was expecting someone dainty and ladylike. He's like a football player with a dress on. Trust me, you do *not* want to mess with him. When they finally got him out of his trailer, tottering about on his wooden geisha shoes, he started in on the wardrobe lady.

"For God's sake, this kimono is like a cheap hotel. There is no ballroom!" He then started grabbing and pulling at his crotch.

Once the wardrobe issues had been handled, he began to pull all kinds of other shenanigans. For one, he refused to get on the horse.

"I'm *not* getting on that horse. I do *not* remember this being in my contract. I am frightened of horses! I'm going back to London *immediately*!"

Then someone from his entourage hollered, "George, be a good fairy and get on the horse!"

"I am a good fairy! Poof! You're a pile of shit! I'm not getting on that horse!"

I explained to him through my heinous monkey mask and fake teeth that this horse was, first of all, not a stallion but a gelding, which meant he'd been neutered, leaving him gentle as a lamb. I told him that the horse's teeth were very long, which meant he was as old as the hills and was not going anywhere in a hurry. And I also said that I had once been a jockey with racehorses and I knew what I was doing. I promised him that I would not let go.

Boy George looked at me, then turned to one of his cohorts and giggled. "She fancies herself a jockey!" he said. He then broke into song: "She'll be comin' 'round the mountain when she comes! She'll be comin' 'round the mountain when she comes!"

It all came to a head during a long shot of us standing majestically atop a high sand dune. The camera was miles away and the director shouted at us through a bullhorn. I had reached the end of my rope. The sand was blowing up under my prosthetic pieces and the skin on my face had been torn to shreds. Both my contact lenses were gritty and dry, and my eyes were hurting beyond belief.

I was so desperate I tearfully asked Boy George what I should do.

"Well, dear, I know a little Japanese," he said. "I'll teach you a phrase so you can alert the director."

"What will I be saying?" I asked, a little suspicious. I could tell he was up to something, but I wasn't sure what.

"I'll teach you how to say 'One more time only.' That'll let the director know you can only handle one more take."

And so he taught me the phrase, which I repeated to anyone who would listen.

Boy George egged me on. "I don't think he heard you. Say it real loud, to that guy over there. He seems to be friends with the director. He'll explain your situation."

What was I saying?

When the interpreter came running over in horror and told me to please shut up, I found out that it was:

"Do you have a big dick?"

Boy George laughed and laughed. Needless to say, I was ignored by the entire Japanese crew for the rest of the shoot.

Spilling My Guts

"Beyond the ideas of wrong-doing and right-doing there is a field.
I'll meet you there." Rumi

The movies are the only business where you can go out
front and applaud yourself.

Will Rogers

I HAVE always thought Gena Rowlands was the
classiest gal around, and here she was, announc-

ing the name of my first screenplay, "Lost in the Pershing Point Hotel," as the winner of the Los Angeles Film Festival's Production Grant Award for 1999! My screenplay had been selected over those of six hundred other applicants, so it was quite an honor.

"Lost in the Pershing Point Hotel" came about from a short story I had written about my days of living on the fringe in Atlanta, Georgia. I had moved to Atlanta when I was nineteen years old so I could live an openly gay life. This was something I had not been able to do even after enrolling in college in Knoxville, an hour away from home. I still bumped into all these people I knew from my church and it was just a mess.

I was tired of living a double life.

Shortly after arriving in Atlanta, I became immersed in the whole 1970s club scene, which involved a lot of drugs and alcohol. I suppose it is human nature to sow a few wild oats in one's impetuous youth, but perhaps because of my small stature I have always felt the need to do things a little bigger than the next person.

I ran amok. With my aberrant behavior and ongoing shenanigans, I put on an exhibition such as the town had never witnessed. I have been told many times that I was a legend. This is not something I am thrilled to admit nowadays, but I suppose the best way to go down is in flames.

Back then, I lived in an old hotel called the Pershing Point Hotel. This Villa Debris was in a dilapidated state and seemed to house many undesirables—there was always a select group of drag queens, thieves, whores, drug pushers, aging strippers, and other riffraff milling about outside. When she came to visit, my mother took one look and refused to get out of the car.

My roommate and main partner in crime during those hairy days was a young woman on the lam from her debutante upbringing. She was a thrift shop peacock in huge black Jackie O sunglasses who strutted around town with everything she owned either on her back or in the enormous bag thrown over her shoulder. She was a self-described "bag lady in a limo."

She was Atlanta's version of Edie Sedgwick.

I called this young woman Miss Make Do. No matter what horrendous situation we found ourselves in—no matter how many times we had to run for our lives, no matter how often the Atlanta police carted us off to jail, no matter how many bars we were unceremoniously thrown out of, or

how many times we were flat broke and hungry—
she was always able to "make do."

I had a sneaking suspicion there was magic
involved, some sort of supernatural phenomenon
she was in touch with.

The short story I wrote dealt with our inabil-
ity to find our apartment. I knew we *had* an apartment. I could prove it. We had slept there on
several occasions. And I had receipts from when,
on the first day of every month, with money we
scraped together—usually by criminal means—I
went to the office of the Pershing Point Hotel and
paid the rent to the enormously fat front desk
clerk, Big Tiny. He peered out from behind a
barred window with a ferocious Chihuahua
named Mitzi Boo in his lap.

The office was easy enough to find (it was
right by the front door), but that damn apartment
of ours was virtually impossible to locate. We
knew it was up a staircase and down a few corri-
dors. But what stairs? Which corridor? We stayed
so high all the time, we were always in a state of
utter confusion.

It is a terrible feeling when you cannot find
your way home.

After an evening of fun and frivolity, Miss

Make Do and I would wander for hours on end, diligently searching for our abode. In between whispered spats, with each of us blaming the other for forgetfulness, we would meander up and down the halls, tottering about on impossibly high platform shoes, trying to not look too conspicuous. When at length we came to the nightly conclusion that we were only going in circles and were not any closer to our destination than when we began our quest, we would fall, exhausted, on the steps in the stairwell.

It was only there that we felt safe. We would camp out till daybreak, smoking cigarettes, rifling through our bags, and trying to get a grip on reality. This is where we spent three years of our young lives. In the stairwell of the Pershing Point Hotel, completely lost.

Eventually Miss Make Do disappeared, and it is anyone's guess where she is today. Years later, when I decided to turn the short story I had written into a theatre piece, I met the perfect actress to play the part of Miss Make Do.

Erin Chandler was the granddaughter of "Happy" Chandler, who had twice been the governor of Kentucky. Between his terms as governor, he had been a U.S. senator and a commissioner of baseball. Erin's father, "Big Dan" Chandler, had fled his Kentucky upbringing for Las Vegas and had run Caesars Palace. Since Erin's parents divorced when she was little, she grew up between Kentucky and Las Vegas.

A blue-blooded Kentucky debutante who had been raised by showgirls?

Hallelujah! I had met my new Miss Make Do! And lucky me. She was a brilliant actress who completely understood and fully embodied her character.

On opening night, a good friend of mine, Jonni Hartman (publicist, mother of the actress Lisa Hartman, and mother-in-law of one of my favorite country-and-western singers, Clint Black) was in the audience. She was with her friend Marilyn Beck, the famous Hollywood columnist, who gave me a lovely write-up in her column.

Both Marilyn Beck and Jonni Hartman told me the same thing: "This is a good play but it would make a wonderful, wonderful screenplay."

I sat down with my good friend Del Shores, the writer-producer-director, and asked for some advice. He told me about several key elements needed in a good screenplay, such as three very distinct "acts," a "hook" to draw the audience in, and so forth. He also suggested a couple of good books on screenwriting. So I went to work. It was all a bit overwhelming but I held tight to Del's best advice: Just make sure to tell the story.

The screenplay floated around town forever and ever. Erin Chandler became the biggest cheerleader for the project and we attached her as both the lead actress and an associate producer. But what we really needed was an executive producer who could raise money. We gave the project to friends of ours who were producers, and they handed it to other friends, but months passed with nothing happening.

It was so disheartening.

Finally the script caught the eyes of a producer named Julia Pierrepont III. We did not know her from Adam's house cat, but she believed so strongly in the piece that she was willing to invest a large sum of her own money. There was one very big stipulation. She wanted to direct the movie, but her only experience as a director had been shooting a few commercials in New York.

She seemed to be a mover and shaker, and her belief in the piece was strong, so we decided to give her a go. The moviemaking business can cause a lot of heartache when friendships are involved. There are people who still do not speak to Erin or me because of our decision to let Julia take the helm. But my goodness, she was able to greenlight the project in a just few months after we had spent almost two years trying to raise the money ourselves. This is a business, after all!

Julia's first question was, How was I going to play myself at nineteen? I was forty-four years old, and all my years of drinking and drug abuse showed on my face. I had never thought about age being a problem, since I had played the part onstage. But camera was not as forgiving.

"Perhaps they could shoot me through cheesecloth?" I asked, tentatively.

"Honey, they'd have to shoot you through burlap," quipped Julia.

Oh dear, I thought. *This is not going well. I don't think I like her and we've just started.*

She suggested finding a younger actor.

I almost blew my stack. "Now, you listen here, Miss Woman. If you think there is another actor on the face of this earth that is going to play *my* part, you have another thing coming."

But Julia was absolutely right. So I sat down and did a rewrite.

I made the lead character in his late thirties—a long stretch, but workable. He was leaving home for the first time in his life. He was going to move to Atlanta and come out of the closet. There are many movies about young people setting out to seek their fortune, but this was going to be about someone doing so much later in life. I felt it really upped the stakes.

Plus there was something really pathetic about a middle-aged man wearing 1970s platform shoes just trying to fit in.

Julia was instrumental in entering the script in the Los Angeles Film Festival's production grant program. When we won the grant, we were given an additional $10,000 on top of what Julia had put in, plus almost $250,000 in free services. This included a free camera, free film, and free time in the editing bay, and even two days' use of a film crane so we could have some really interesting shots.

This was all well and good, but what we needed was more money. We did not have nearly enough to shoot the picture. We decided that it would be necessary to get letters of intent from famous people to help us get our funding. We were able to round up all kinds of stars to do cameos: John Ritter, Marilu Henner, Kathy Kinney, and Sheryl Lee Ralph, plus Michelle Phillips from the Mamas & the Papas. I didn't want to have to do that, but having those famous people attached helped raise a few dollars. For the rest of the money, we begged, we borrowed, we stole, we scammed, we maxed out credit cards, we did anything we could think of to secure funds.

I even stooped to sucking a few cocks to obtain some cash. This is not something I am particularly proud of, but what can I say? I was born without a gag reflex and I'm pretty good at it. Welcome to Hollywood. What's your dream?

Only kidding! Actually, I did volunteer my services but there were no takers. Even when I promised to take my teeth out.

I'm kidding!

My teeth don't come out.

In the early part of June 1999, on Julia Pierrepont's ranch out in Calabasas, California, we began principal photography on *Lost in the Pershing Point Hotel*. We had less than $285,000 in the kitty. In movie terms, that is not low budget, it is *no* budget.

What a journey! It almost killed all of us. And

there was a lot of bad behavior involved. Most of it on my part.

I think we had maybe twenty-two days to shoot a full-length feature film. Besides Julia's ranch, we had secured the entire Ambassador Hotel on Wilshire Boulevard, the hotel where Robert F. Kennedy had been assassinated. It had been empty since the 1970s. The kitchen area where Kennedy had been shot was bricked off, but the ballroom where he had given his final speech was just as it had been on that fateful day. The hotel was old and musty, plus it was home to feral animals that roamed the halls and made all kinds of horrific noises when we were shooting at night. But it made the perfect location, as our film was a "period piece" and therefore very little set decoration was required. That turned out to be a godsend for our low-budget production.

The very first day on the set I realized that my vision and Julia's vision were radically different. I saw *Lost in the Pershing Point Hotel* as a comedy. She saw it as an intense cautionary tale about drug abuse. I wanted light and frothy; she wanted dark and shadowy. I wanted Rock Hudson and Doris Day run amok, she wanted "Drugstore Fucking Cowboy." She wanted long sweeping camera shots with very little coverage and I wanted my goddamn close-up!

I especially did not want the drug use to overshadow the lovely message of a gay man's search for himself. To me, this was not a piece about drug use but a piece about how gay people sometimes use drugs to deal with the shame of their homosexuality.

We fought tooth and nail on almost everything. It was horrendous. We were constantly at each other's throat. Poor Erin Chandler had to run interference as the producer instead of concentrating on her own performance. Then she would jump into the fray.

I remember at one point screaming in Julia's face, "This is my fucking life story. I have been kicked around this goddamn town for a hundred fucking years. This is my one shot at the big time and you're fucking it up! You can get a lot of things back in Hollywood Town but you cannot get back your REP-U-TA-TION! And mine is at stake here!"

To which she calmly replied, "Please remember that I have given up my life savings, I lost a baby, I'm going to lose my ranch, and I am very close to also losing my husband. So, please, sweetheart, do not come crying to me about your lost reputation."

Passive-aggressive behavior really pisses me off. She would not even give me the satisfaction of a good screaming match.

To say that I was an ungrateful little shit would be putting it mildly.

I pitched fit after fit after fit. I was like a Tasmanian Devil. I could not help myself. I would head to the hotel every morning, sometimes with only a few hours sleep, swearing to myself that I was going to be a good boy. Within a few minutes of arriving I would be off on a rant. The hallowed halls of the Ambassador Hotel rang loudly with my bellowing.

The crew took to yelling "Thar she blows!"

And all of this was after two years of complete sobriety. How embarrassing!

My spiritual advisor suggested that before opening my mouth to scream at Julia, I take a minute and ask myself three important questions about what I was about to say: Is it kind? Is it true? Is it necessary?

Well, my goodness gracious, that would have rendered me *mute*.

So I ignored his advice.

I have since learned from working with many alcoholics in early recovery that just because the booze and drugs have been taken away does not mean the anger is gone. It has been my experience that it usually intensifies during early sobriety. As a newly recovered alcoholic, I had not yet acquired the tools needed to deal with my anger. This usually takes years and years of going to meetings and doing the recovery work. A person who has always dealt with life's problems by having a drink has no earthly idea what to do when anger—a lot of which comes from not being able to have a drink!—rears its ugly head.

Somehow we made it through the torturous shoot, and the film wrapped on June 22, 1999. At the first screening, my agent, Billy Miller, leaned in to me and whispered, "What a beautiful, glorious . . . mess."

Julia had made a really stunning picture. Her shots were interesting and very pretty to look at. Her use of color gave the picture a big-budget look. She had hired a lady who had done some editing for the famous German filmmaker Rainer Werner Fassbinder, so the picture moved along nicely. The glowering problem was that somehow the story had gotten lost.

There was no story. It really was a mess.

My agent said, "Leslie, I have no idea what this film is about. Plus, this film is dependent upon the audience liking you and we don't see enough of you as there are very few close-ups."

AHA! See? *See?* I was now going to get my revenge. I told that bitch a long time ago that I wanted my close-up!

But there was very little time for that. Julia, Erin, and I huddled out at the ranch in Calabasas for days and days. We finally came up with a good fix. To this day we still argue over who actually came up with the idea, but all that is irrelevant because I know who came up with it. Me.

We decided to put my drug overdose at the beginning of the film instead of at the end. We then raised an additional sixty grand and rented a studio for one day of reshoots. In the studio we built a beautiful all-white room, with billowing white curtains, a perfect white table with a perfect white vase holding a perfect white calla lily, and a perfect white chair sitting upon a perfect white rug.

When the drug overdose happens at the beginning of the film—*BAM!*—I land in the white room. The audience quickly ascertains that this is Gay Purgatory, where God keeps homosexuals until he decides what to do with them. Throughout the film I intermittently argue my case to a perfect white light as I sit in the perfect white room in a perfect white suit.

Essentially, I tell my story to God.

And it worked. The film now worked!

We took *Lost in the Pershing Point Hotel* on a long film festival circuit. Erin, Julia, and I carried our precious baby in an enormous film canister all over the country. We had only one copy of our film. It would have cost an additional four grand for another one and we were tapped, so we made do with one copy. We were too embarrassed to explain this to film festival coordinators, and so it was sometimes a nightmare crisscrossing the country trying to make all those festivals, lugging our one-and-only ragged copy of the film.

At some film festivals, especially the gay and lesbian ones, we were a hit. But at some others we were completely ignored. Sometimes the reviews were good, sometimes they weren't. We had an awful time getting distribution. Every once in a while we would get someone to try to shepherd us through the process, but after about a year, our sad film canister ended up sitting in Erin's closet.

We eventually secured a tiny distribution deal that at least got the movie into most major movie-rental stores. It certainly wasn't what we envisioned. Just the other day at Amoeba Records up on Sunset Boulevard I saw a copy of our precious, precious baby in the Three for Ten Dollars bin.

Three for ten dollars? Apparently that is what my life story is worth. I wanted to cry. It was all just heartbreaking. No one sets out to make a bad picture, and *Lost in the Pershing Point Hotel* was certainly not a bad picture. It was a picture that did not quite know what it was, and never found its audience.

It was a beautiful, glorious . . . mess.

What I was left with were memories of some really bad behavior. And what bothered me most was that this was not the first time I'd been through this. My experience on *Lost in the Pershing Point Hotel* mirrored what I had gone through years before, with my first one-man show, *Hysterical Blindness and Other Southern Tragedies That Have Plagued My Life Thus Far.*

My first mentor in Hollywood was Carolyne Barry, the energetic owner of an acting school originally called the Professional Artists Group. I

met Carolyne a day after stepping off the bus in
Los Angeles. She was instrumental in helping me
find a lucrative career in commercials. She also
taught me the important lesson that "show business" is two words, and "business" is the more important one. I learned to treat my quest to become
a working actor as a business. This worked wonderfully paired with the training I had received
under Fred Beranger, my first mentor. Dr. Beranger headed up the Department of Theatre at
the University of Tennessee at Chattanooga, and
he had taught me a great reverence for the craft of
acting, but not a whole lot about how to earn a
living at it.

Carolyne Barry was also instrumental in taking my first one-man show from her living room
all the way to a seven-month run Off-Broadway
in New York. She directed and shaped the show
from day one.

And how did I repay her? By acting like
something out of *The Bad Seed*!

I was a tiny terrorist nightmare.

Even to this day, when we do bump into each
other, Carolyne and I are very polite and friendly,
but the scars from that experience are so deep
I don't think I will ever be able to fully make

amends. And I know that we can never have the deep friendship we enjoyed before we took our show to New York.

It is all so sad. We are taught in recovery to not regret the wreckage of our past, but it still hurts. What is interesting is that I am such an accommodating actor for hire, when my own words are not involved. Directors love me. Directors hire me over and over because they know I can be counted on to deliver the goods with very little extraneous drama. This is of utmost importance in television work, where there is just not time for any bullshit.

But when it is something I have written myself, I walk around loaded for bear, as we say in the South. Perhaps it is because my writings are always so damn personal. I learned at the age of seventeen, when I first began writing in a journal, that when I wrote about stuff going on in my life, it helped me sort it all out. If I read what I had written aloud to another person, it really helped me gain clarity. And when I realized that I had a talent for standing onstage and telling stories about my life, and could do it in a really entertaining (and lucrative) manner, my demons truly began to let me go free.

And I have learned over the years from thousands and thousands of letters and e-mails, and the response from people after my shows, that whatever I am doing is a good thing. So I have quit wondering why I spill my guts.

The problem I had with Carolyne—as with Julia Pierrepont—was that my vision of the piece was very different from hers. She had a strong personality and I constantly felt like I was losing my show. It was *my* story of growing up in the Southern Baptist church. It was *my* story of growing up gay in the Deep South. It was *my* story of dealing with my mother's psychosomatic illness, hysterical blindness. It was about the death of my father and all that the death entailed. It was the story of my twin sisters and some of their troubles. I was even going to trot out my mother's disastrous second marriage—to my stepmonster.

It was all just too much.

My mother is an intensely private woman and I was tossing out the family's dirty laundry for the whole world to see and to laugh at. I knew she would be incredibly upset, so I was freaking out constantly.

And I took it out on Carolyne.

She once took me aside and told me a heartbreaking story involving her parents and their habit of sometimes bickering in public. She asked me nicely to please not scream at her in front of the cast as it brought back terrible memories and literally made her want to break down and sob. I did not listen to a word she said. My anger was unmanageable.

Finally, the show was about to open Off-Broadway, and my mother insisted on coming and bringing my favorite aunt. I had to make the dreaded phone call. I called my mother in Tennessee and laid my cards on the table. I told her everything that was in the play.

There was a long, dead silence.

"Leslie Allen Jordan. Do you mean to tell me that you are going to stand onstage in New York City and just talk about *all that*?"

"Yes, ma'am. I am going to sing about it, too."

Carolyne had added a Baptist choir to stand behind me. The choir functioned as a Greek chorus. As I told my stories, the choir members became all the other characters. They were the voices in my head, the voices from my past. There were also eleven original songs that my dear friend Joe Patrick Ward had written. It was the most

overpopulated one-man show since Shirley Mac-
Laine hit the Pantages Theater in Los Angeles.

There was one line that I knew would probably cause my mother and my aunt to faint. Taken
out of the context of the play, it sounds risqué, but
it was delivered at a point when I am trying desperately to reconcile my devout Baptist upbringing with my homosexuality.

"Let's face it, it's hard, it's hard to be a good
Christian *and a cocksucker too!*"

I worried myself sick. I considered dropping
the line, but it was the big showstopper. I did not
think it would be fair to the other audience members. Besides, what if there were critics in the
house? That line was important.

At last I hit upon a solution.

I discreetly bought the four seats surrounding
my mother and my aunt. I got four friends to sit
in those seats. We practiced and practiced until
the four of them were able to simultaneously
cough loudly at the exact moment I said "cocksucker."

To this day, when asked about the New York
fiasco where she had to endure the torment of her
whole life paraded out onstage, my mother only
says, "Well, I missed the big laugh. I'm not sure I

even want to know what it was, but both my sister and I missed the big laugh."

My mother is of the opinion that if you can't say something nice about something it's best to not say anything at all. She rarely mentions *Hysterical Blindness and Other Southern Tragedies That Have Plagued My Life Thus Far.*

I have quite a history with the word "cocksucker." My second one-man show, *Like a Dog on Linoleum,* also used that word. I peeped my head out of the curtain once when I was performing in Los Angeles and there was Reba McEntire with her husband, Narvel Blackstock. I almost tossed my cookies. I had a cute, reccurring character on Reba's sitcom and had fallen in love with her. Everyone falls in love with Reba. She is just that kind of gal. Her show was the only show I had ever worked on in Hollywood that had a prayer circle before going in front of the studio audience. The prayer circle certainly wasn't a requirement, but anyone who wanted to join in was invited. It always had a lovely interdenominational prayer and gave the cast a real sense of purpose.

How on earth was I going to say "cocksucker" in front of Reba? I had prayed with her just a week before!

I came running onstage and began the show. I could not take my eyes off Reba and Narvel. I should not have been worried. They laughed and laughed, especially Reba. She laughed hardest at the naughtiest parts! They may be fairly conservative but, come on, they are in show business. Half of Reba's writing staff were gay men.

And afterwards, Narvel, Reba's very masculine, very straight husband, paid me an amazing compliment.

"Every straight guy in America should hear your story," he said.

I was moved beyond words.

When I finally got sober and was told that it was very important to make amends to anyone in my past that I had hurt, Carolyne Barry was near the top of the list. I knew that a letter saying "I am sorry" would not be enough in this case. So I tried being inventive. Carolyne has continued to teach over the years and is brilliant at what she does. I began to send her students. Over the years I have probably recommended her acting class to a hundred people. It is the least I can do.

Celebrity Crushes

I HAVE been blessed with a deep appreciation for beauty. I think that's why homosexuals were put on this earth—to make things pretty. I love to be around beautiful things, and that is why I love to be around Mark Harmon.

Mark Harmon is a walking work of art. He is absolutely breathtaking. And he is, may I add, aging like fine wine. I worked with Mark and Marlee Matlin on the TV series *Reasonable Doubts* in the early 1990s, and then had the pleasure of being directed by him years later on *Boston Public*.

The first time I worked with Mark Harmon, I thought I was going to faint. Seldom are we mortals allowed to be in the presence of such godlike creatures. Mark and I had a stakeout scene together. My character talked incessantly, to the point where Mark's character, in desperation, was supposed to throw me to the floor, straddle me, and tape my mouth shut.

The director yelled "Action!" and Mark threw me to the floor, straddled me, and began to tape my mouth shut. Before he got it completely taped, I was supposed to yell out the next line. But as I gazed up at that flawless face, I couldn't speak. His physical beauty rendered me mute.

The director said, "Leslie, you have the next line."

"I know, I know. I'm sorry. Can we go again?"

So once again, Mark threw me to the floor, straddled me, and began to tape my mouth shut. Oh dear. I gazed up at all that loveliness and I could not speak.

"Do you need the script supervisor to read you the line?" the director asked, exasperated.

"No, no. I know the line. I'm terribly sorry. Could we just go again? Please."

Round three. As Mark put his face near mine to apply the tape, I noticed a tiny scar somewhere in the vicinity of his right eye. It was just a tiny little flaw. But it was so endearing.

I fell hopelessly in love.

The director was at his wits' end. "Damn it, Leslie, what is the problem? How long are we going to have to do the fucking scene over and over?"

"I don't know what's wrong with me. I'm so sorry."

It was at that point that Mark leaned in and whispered, "I think I know what you're up to."

He was on to me! He knew I loved being manhandled! The horror and humiliation began to sink in. I sputtered, but nothing of any consequence would come out. Then something amazing happened. He laughed. What a wonderful, hearty laugh! I began to laugh, too.

The poor director just threw up his hands.

Mark stood up and joked to the director as I lay prostrate on the floor in a fit of giggles. "I have a deaf woman and a trick dog to deal with. And now this!"

. . .

Speaking of beauty, I once had the enormous pleasure of working with George Clooney. We did sixteen episodes of the television series *Bodies of Evidence* together. This was years before George became a big star. There is no one on this planet that deserves success more than he does. George Clooney has paid his dues. He has been around forever. He has been around almost as long as I have. George once told me he had twelve television series under his belt.

Only twelve? Including pilots that were shot but not aired, I have had fifteen series regular roles. I have been in so many failed television shows I always feel the need to apologize to the cast in advance.

"This show had a shot but . . . they hired me. Sorry!"

What a business.

I get so tickled when I hear people making a big fuss over George. When I see him portrayed as the suave, sophisticated ladies' man, I think, *Huh*? Yes, George always gets the girl. But he gets the girl because he's the class clown. He's always cutting up and carrying on. George has this enormous capacity for happiness, and it is infectious.

I loved working with George. And he's easy on the eyes, that's for sure. Oh, what a crush I had on George. He knew it, too. He had me running myself ragged to do his bidding.

Bodies of Evidence was a big-city-detective show and the only show I've ever been cast in where I was not allowed to be funny. I played a forensic detective.

"Wouldn't it be funny if I tripped over my bag and fell as I was collecting fiber samples?" I asked.

"Mr. Jordan, just say the line, please, and do the business as directed."

I had started this low-fat diet and I talked about it incessantly. I suppose George heard about it, because he went to the wardrobe people and secretly told them to pull an inch out of the waist of the pants I wore on the show every day. I would show up for work, get in costume, and harp to anyone who would listen how my diet was working so miraculously.

"Oh, look y'all!" I would shout gleefully as I stretched out the waistband of my pants as proof. "I weigh the same every morning, but I guess this diet makes you lose inches, because look at this, y'all. Look!"

By the third or fourth day, I was cinching my pants with an enormous belt and practically skipping all around the set because I thought I was getting so skinny. When I found out about George's deception, I confronted him. He laughed and laughed. He swears to this day that he was not the culprit.

Aunt Matt

When I need a good laugh there are a couple of people I call. One person is my dear friend Jane Abbott, who is intrinsically one of the funniest people alive. She definitely has the gift. So when I am feeling down, I call her up and beg her to tell me "that funny fart story."

I am always up for a good fart story.

Oh, lighten up! Farts are funny. Rude noises are funny. Situations created from a bad smell are funny. And in this day and age of constant turmoil and strife, I'm up for anything that gives me a chuckle.

Jane Abbott was raised in Dallas, and she is a Texas gal through and through. When she starts spinning a yarn, I feel like I'm back where I belong. Even though she's from Texas and I'm from Tennessee, there's something about her vocal patterns and how she knows the right place to pause to get the desired effect that takes me home.

When Jane was growing up in the 1950s, her favorite person in the whole wide world was her aunt Matt. Aunt Matt was known as "the town character." Everybody in town knew her. She was a large woman who raised chickens for a living. She wore dungarees twenty years before it was fashionable for women—she'd wear them right up under her big, blousy, homemade housedress. Aunt Matt's bra straps were always flapping down her big, fleshy arms, and she wore men's brogans.

A large woman with a man's name who loves the outdoors, and who wears blue jeans and men's shoes? It sounds to me like Aunt Matt was a lesbian way ahead of her time. Now, Jane has certainly never mentioned Aunt Matt's sexual preference. That is something a well-brought-up gal from Texas just wouldn't do. It is just a thought of mine.

It was Jane's job when she was a little girl to go down to the chicken yard once a week. She'd go running to and fro all around the yard chasing the baby chickens. When she caught them, she put them in a shoe box, which had holes poked in the top so they could breathe.

Once Jane had a full load, she and her beloved Aunt Matt would walk up the long driveway to the highway, shoe box in hand, catch the county bus, and take a ride into town to sell the chicks at the local farmers' market. After the chicks were sold, Jane was treated to an afternoon at the picture show.

One balmy summer Texas morning they sat side by side, riding the bumpy bus into town. All of a sudden, the bus hit a big pothole and—*BAM!*—that shoebox went flying through the air. Moments later, baby chickens were running up and down the aisles. The bus driver almost veered into a ditch while looking in the rearview mirror to see what the commotion was all about.

Aunt Matt heaved herself forward, lumbering up and down the aisle, calling out in a low singsong voice, "Here, chickie, chickie! Here, chickie, chickie, chick!"

The other passengers watched intently, and they all tried to stifle their giggles as Aunt Matt's big ass made its way up the aisle. Jane was at the age, around eleven or twelve, when she was beginning to realize that Aunt Matt was something of a spectacle. Jane loved her aunt dearly but was becoming embarrassed by Aunt Matt's odd ways of dressing and acting. As she sat there watching Aunt Matt all bent over trying to catch the baby chickens, she wanted to crawl into a hole and disappear.

And then it happened.

Aunt Matt farted.

Not once. Not twice. But three times! Right there in the middle of the bus. Jane was absolutely mortified. She told me she's been haunted by the sound of those farts to this very day. She said they sounded like gunfire.

Now, in the back of the bus sat an old cowboy with a mouth full of chewing tobacco. When Aunt Matt cut the cheese, that old cowboy just about blew a gasket.

He let out a huge war whoop, and yelled, "That's right, Aunt Matt. If you can't catch them chickens, *shoot 'em*!

Genghis Cowboys

I am just an ingénue and shall be till I'm eighty-two!
Noël Coward

I HAVE a friend named Austin Hanks who hails from LA. Lower Alabama, that is. He is a tall, gorgeous drink of water covered in tattoos. He can sing like an angel, play the guitar like the Devil, and spin a yarn that will hold you spellbound. He is sweet as cherry pie.

I first met him at a Chinese restaurant where he used to perform on the second Tuesday of every month. The restaurant is called Genghis Cohen, and it sits in the middle of Hollywood, on Melrose Avenue. It hosted a showcase for up-and-coming Southern musicians called "It Came from Nashville."

I never missed a Tuesday for years and years.

I would arrive early, have a big plate of Queen's Chicken (naturally), then move into the showcase lounge, sit in the front row, and adore Austin Hanks.

When I need a laugh and Jane Abbott's stories won't do the trick, I know who to call. I beg Austin to tell me about his grandmother back in Alabama. Everyone called her Mamaw. She was hard of hearing and had a terrible habit of mixing up words.

One night, the whole family was gathered at the dinner table.

"Mamaw, this roast is delicious," Austin hollered.

"Well, it ought to be," wailed Mamaw. "I urinated it all night long."

Another time, it was the day after the big Fourth of July festivities.

"You look tired, Mamaw. Did you not sleep good?" Austin asked.

"Who could," yelled Mamaw, "with them kids throwing Roman Catholics up against the wall all night?"

"Roman *candles,* Mamaw!"

Someone had once bought Mamaw a bottle of

shampoo that she really liked, but she could not remember the name. "What's that shampoo called?" she would ask repeatedly.

"It's called Pantene, Mamaw."

Well, one night over dinner, someone complimented Mamaw on her hairdo.

She smiled broadly. "I been washing it with that poontang!"

In the South we do not put crazy people away—we put them out on the porch so everyone can enjoy them!

Another time, I looked up at the stage at Genghis Cohen and almost swooned. There was this boy named Travis Howard singing a song he wrote called "Ruby Falls." I felt like he had written it just for me. Ruby Falls is a real cheesy tourist attraction on Lookout Mountain near Chattanooga, Tennessee. We used to go there all the time when we were kids. It was a child's wonderland. Concrete gnomes! A cave called Fat Man's Squeeze! And all kinds of fairy statues and such. I guess I was easily amused.

Travis Howard was full-lipped and fine-figured. He wore his ripped Levi's jeans real tight.

He had a butt you could serve tea on. I had never seen a butt like that on a straight boy. It bordered on the obscene.

I went home, sat down, and wrote him a love letter. I knew he was straight (and half my age), but I couldn't help myself. In the letter, I told him he reminded me of a Hindu deity. He was like something "not of this world," like a beautiful, guitar-playing Lord Krishna, the Blue God. I told him such beauty needed to be recognized and I felt sure he was going to make it big. And I would be his fan till the day I died.

I don't know what came over me, gushing and simpering like that. And to make matters worse, I sent flowers! What was I thinking? I found out he was appearing at a club called the Gig and I sent the flowers with my love letter attached.

The next night, I was in the dressing room of the Zephyr Theatre, getting ready to go onstage in a play called *Southern Baptist Sissies*. The stage manager brought me a note. Travis Howard was waiting in a restaurant across the street and asked if I would care to join him after my performance.

I screamed and locked myself in the bathroom.

I could barely contain myself. I sat on the toilet in full stage makeup with my costume on, reading and rereading his note. I thought I was going to fall apart. I've decided almost all gay men my age have what I call "Marilyn Monroe syndrome." We love to fall apart. We love to take pills and cry and carry on. We love self-created drama.

The stage manager didn't know what was going on. He had no idea what was in the note he handed me. He thought someone had died.

I have to admit that my performance in *Southern Baptist Sissies* suffered that night. It was all I could do to get my lines out. My mind was already across the street with the beautiful young Travis Howard.

After the curtain fell, I ran across the street. I thought he was the most stunning man alive. He was so flattered by my attentions, and he told me that gay men had been coming on to him for years and he considered it a huge compliment.

He told me that back home in Georgia, where he grew up, everyone thought he and his best friend were gay because they hung out together all the time, and both loved Christian music and were not very good at sports. One time, his daddy walked into the bedroom and just flat out asked Travis's best friend if he was a homosexual. Travis almost fell over.

Without missing a beat, Travis's friend said, "Well, Mr. Howard, I don't think so. Why? Are you asking me out on a date? Because if I was gay, I don't think I'd date older men."

Travis's daddy turned red and walked out of the room without saying a word.

Travis Howard and I talked deep into the night. We struck up an amazing friendship that has lasted to this day. He appeared on *Nashville Star,* which is sort of the country-and-western version of *American Idol.* He didn't win, but he met another amazing singer named Miranda Lambert. He writes a lot of her songs and is often on the road for months at a time. I miss him. I miss my beautiful, straight, guitar-playing friend with a butt you could serve tea on.

One of my most memorable nights at Genghis Cohen, a young man named Waylon Payne took the stage. I discovered that he was the namesake of Waylon Jennings and was the son of Sammi Smith.

Well.

Miss Smith was a country music legend who had a huge crossover hit in the 1970s with the Kris Kristofferson song "Help Me Make It Through the Night." I loved that song. I loved her husky voice. I played that record over and over until I wore the grooves out.

Now here was Miss Smith's son in the flesh!

He looked just like a skinny James Dean. Years later, I went to see *Walk the Line,* the movie about Johnny Cash, and there was Waylon Payne, playing a young Jerry Lee Lewis!

The first night I laid eyes on Waylon Payne, it was like seeing a sad, skinny puppy that I wanted to take home and feed. He sure was named appropriately—he really was "wailin' pain." He had the ability to infuse every song he sang with such angst, you almost had to lay down and rest afterwards.

Someone from the crowd yelled out for him to sing his mother's signature song. I suppose the patron had no idea that Sammi Smith had recently died, and it had torn Waylon to pieces. I held my breath. Waylon hesitated. Was he going to sing it or not? He shut his eyes and strummed a chord. I shut my eyes, too.

Could this be happening? The son of Miss

Sammi Smith? Time stood still. Waylon's high tenor brought his mama's song to life.

In the Southern Baptist church, there is always a group of women who cry all the way through the testimonials. They are affectionately called "sob sisters." When Waylon started singing his mama's song, I became a sob sister. Yes, ma'am, tears were streaming down my face. I thought my heart was going to burst out of my chest. I began to sob harder and sing along.

I was not alone.

I wanted to stand before the crowd and give my testimony: "Ain't it the truth, people! Don't we all? Don't we all just need a friend?"

At that point in the song, Waylon sang just like his mama did in her version. He got real soft, so soft you could barely hear him. He put his guitar aside and whispered the words. We all leaned forward in anticipation.

"I don't want to be alone. Help me make it through the . . . night."

The place went ape shit.

Right after that, Levi Kreis, who hails from Knoxville, Tennessee, jumped onstage and tore into a rousing rendition of "Will the Circle Be Unbroken?" Levi is a tall, skinny white boy, but when he opens his mouth to sing, Mahalia Jackson pops out. His singing could make a Pentecostal put on lipstick!

It became a free-for-all.

We sang every hymn in the Baptist hymnal that night. The drunker we got, the more we sang. Hymn after hymn after hymn. By the time we reached "The Old Rugged Cross," even the Jews were singing and clapping along.

I am here to tell you, it was a night to remember.

Under the Brilliant Pen

Conventional wisdom teaches us that creativity requires rigid discipline. The reality is that creativity requires consistent attentive compassion.

Julia Cameron, *The Artist's Way*

I'VE BEEN extremely blessed to have worked with some of the best writers in television. I learned early in my career that film is a director's medium, stage is an actor's medium, and television is a writer's medium. So to have been chosen by all these amazing television writers has been a real source of pride.

I have worked on and off with David E. Kelley for years. And do you know, I have never even met him? Well, that is not exactly true—he once poked his head in the door, waved, and gave us all the thumbs-up during a table read of *Boston Public*.

But he and I have never spoken a word to each other. This is probably a good thing. Knowing my track record with handsome straight men, I would more than likely have developed an angst-ridden crush on him, had he even glanced in my direction. And my simmering resentment of his beautiful wife, Michelle Pfeiffer, would have been exhausting.

One of Mr. Kelley's producers (and a dear friend of mine), Alice West, saw me in *Southern Baptist Sissies* and brought me in to audition for an episode of *Ally McBeal*. I was to play a cloning expert named Dr. Benjamin Harris. All of my scenes were with Robert Downey Jr. I had recently spent a little time in the slammer with him, so it was a reunion of sorts. (There will be more on my unfortunate incarceration later.)

After the episode aired, my agent called and

told me I must have scored a coup, because Mr. Kelley was writing me into another episode. An unknown actor and singer named Josh Groban had been hired to play a high school student who wanted to sue his prom date because she backed out at the last minute. I played Josh Groban's choir teacher, Dr. Benjamin Harris, cloning expert / church choir director.

Josh Groban was about nine feet tall. He was a sweet, gangly kid, but as soon as he opened his mouth to sing, he became a swan before my very eyes. It was like magic. What a crush I had on young Josh Groban!

Over the summer, I was cast in David E. Kelley's new show, *Boston Public,* to do five episodes as a science teacher. I became Dr. Benjamin Harris, cloning expert / church choir director / science teacher. One of the early episodes of *Boston Public* involved my character encouraging his students to do a gay version of Thornton Wilder's famous play *Our Town.* The gay version was called *Our Town Too.* It caused a huge stink, as it involved a smoking-hot lesbian kiss between two students. I was now Dr. Benjamin Harris, cloning expert / church choir director / science teacher / drama teacher / gay activist.

Then, apparently to send my character out on a high note, in my final episode of *Boston Public* I went online and talked dirty with some of my female students. I was caught and dismissed. In true David E. Kelley fashion, the teachers' union intervened and took the principal to court, and I got to keep my job. But my character soon realized that word of his disgrace had spread among the student population, and he would never truly regain their respect. I quit, and walked away with my head held high as Dr. Benjamin Harris, cloning expert / church choir director / science teacher / drama teacher / gay activist / heterosexual pedophile.

My real journey under the brilliant pen of David E. Kelley began when I was cast in *Boston Legal*. I played a murderer who was so darn nice, the people around the law firm had to keep reminding themselves that I was indeed a murderer. I killed my mother by bopping her on the head with a skillet. I then killed a neighbor in the same fashion. Then, in a beautifully engineered turn of events, Miss Betty White bopped me on the head with a skillet.

Bless her sweet heart! Betty White was con-

cerned about hitting me with a skillet. I showed
her that it was made of rubber, not cast iron, and
I gave her permission to give me a real hard wallop so it would look good on camera. I had been
given several furniture pads stacked on top of one
another in case I fell.

The director called "Action!"

Betty White hauled off and smacked the beje-
sus out of me. I flew out of my chair, sailed past
where the furniture pads were placed, and landed
unceremoniously on the soundstage floor with the
wind knocked out of me. Betty White was horri-
fied, and I had to pretend it didn't hurt at all. But
it hurt like hell. I saw stars! In her eighties, Betty
White still packs quite a wallop.

I assumed my character on the show had died,
until my agent called with news that they needed
me back.

"Perhaps they're keeping me around?" I
asked, hopeful.

Nope. But Betty White was going to keep me
locked in a freezer for the next couple of episodes.
So I spent several hours with my lips painted blue,
covered in itchy fake ice crystals and lying on a
wooden board in an unplugged freezer. Once I
was loaded into the freezer, I could not get out,

since camera equipment blocked the door. As I lay there, I noticed that I was half hidden with TV dinners that were covered in fake frost.

What was the name on the boxes?

Freezer Queen!

So I surreptitiously placed the fake TV dinners all around my face. Just a little joke for the boys in the back room!

There is a mistaken notion that Los Angeles is a theatrical wasteland. This could not be farther from the truth. Trust me, theatre is alive and well and flourishing in Los Angeles. I am convinced that stage experience is what sets the really great actors apart from the good actors. It is very easy in film and television to act "from the neck up." It is truly amazing what can be done in the editing bay with an awful acting performance on film. I have worked with actors who were believed to be at the top of their craft and immediately realized on the set that their entire careers were made in the editing bay.

The writer to whom I owe most of my career is Del Shores. Although Del has written for many television shows, including *Queer as Folk, Dharma & Greg,* and *Ned and Stacy,* he is best known for his enormously successful plays. All of his plays take place in his home state of Texas and are known for eliciting both gut-wrenching laughter and heartrending moments of truth. Almost every acting job I have been hired to do can somehow be traced back to my appearance in one of Del Shores's plays.

I had heard that his first play, *Cheatin'* (which I saw five times before I even met Del), was holding auditions at a dinner theatre in Kansas City. I had been in Los Angeles only a few years at that point, but had been lucky enough to get into two of the three actors' unions: the Screen Actors Guild and the American Federation of Television and Radio Artists. I also wanted to get into Actors' Equity, the stage union, and this seemed like the perfect opportunity. I went in to audition for the part of Bo Bob Jasper, a dim-witted, love-struck mailman. I walked into the room and delivered the first line.

"Mornin', Sid. Nice day, ain't it."

Del Shores almost fell off the couch. He laughed all the way through my audition. I was hired on the spot and he has not stopped laughing—at me and with me—for almost twenty years.

Del, who is now openly gay, was engaged to a woman back then. Kelly Alexander was the daughter of Newel Alexander, who, like myself, had appeared in all of Del's plays. We were one big huge family of displaced Southerners who relied on one another for love and support.

I was asked to be a member of Del and Kelly's wedding party. When their first daughter, Rebecca, was born, I was asked to be the godfather. Del Shores was my "straight" friend for ten years. We spoke three times a day on the phone.

I have always considered my "gaydar" to be excellent. I can spot a fellow homo at forty paces. But never once did it cross my mind that Del might be homosexual. He is very masculine, and back then, like all good Texas boys, he wore Wrangler jeans and cowboy boots. He is the son of a Southern Baptist preacher and had graduated from a big Baptist college in Waco, Texas.

In retrospect, I think he was a little too interested in my sexual shenanigans. This was years before I got sober, so my drunken, drug-addled sex life was like a soap opera unto itself. I do not think most straight men would want the details.

Trust me, Del Shores wanted details.

I had once gotten drunk, taken some pills

for my nerves, and had a bad reaction. I somehow passed out inside the gates of a lumberyard that sits among all the gay bars in the middle of West Hollywood. How I got inside the gates of this lumberyard is anyone's guess—but the really horrific part of the story is that when I got home, I realized *I did not have on any underpants.*

When I told Del, he kept pressing me for more information.

"What do you think happened?" he asked.

"Delferd, I don't know what happened. I got home and I was not wearing any underpants."

"Well, think hard! Think back real hard!"

"I don't know."

"It's a wonder they didn't press charges for *trespassing*!" Del exclaimed. "Do you think you had hot, steamy, homosexual sex on a forklift?"

But back then I did not think twice about his sexuality.

When he called to tell me the sad news that he and Kelly had separated, I was at a loss for words.

"Leslie, I just cannot live this lie one more minute," Del said. "I am a homosexual. I've known it forever. But because of my whole religious upbringing I could not bring myself to admit it. It is not fair to Kelly. I always thought it was something that would go away, but it has not. And I feel like my whole life is a lie."

The only thing I could think to say was, "Oh, honey, we are going to have so much fun!"

He told me years later that remark brought him a lot of comfort during those dark days. The divorce was horrendous. We were all so close. We all tried our best to not take sides, but I felt caught in the middle because I was Del's only gay friend at the time. I had to lend him the most support as I was the only one who truly understood what it meant to come out.

The only ones who seemed to take it all in stride were the ones we worried about the most: Del and Kelly's daughters. They were six and four at the time. I remember once, right after the divorce, the girls wanted to get a hamburger at Carl's Jr. Del pulled the car over to explain why we couldn't eat at Carl's Jr. I thought they were a little young to have any kind of understanding of the whole ordeal, but Del was adamant about explaining everything.

"Girls, remember what I explained to you about being gay."

The girls were sitting in the back seat, bored

stiff. They nodded their heads, looked out the window, and chomped their gum.

"Well, there was this gay girl named Ellen. And Ellen had a television show that was very popular. When Ellen came out and told everyone she was gay, Carl's Jr. pulled their advertising. So I don't think we should give them our money."

The four-year-old, Caroline, sat there twirling her hair.

Finally she said, "Well, thank God it wasn't McDonald's."

I am not proud of the fact that I was not around a lot during Rebecca and Caroline's formative years. I was too busy drinking, doing drugs, and running around on the streets of Hollywood. But I sobered up, turned around, and there they stood: grown, accomplished, confident young women. They are both wonderfully nonjudgmental and they seem to take everything in stride. They have an amazing relationship with Kelly, Del, and Del's longtime partner, Jason, who once flew eighteen hours all the way to Japan to see Madonna on the last leg of her world tour.

How cool is that?

Itty-Bitty

WHEN I was growing up in the hills of Tennessee, all of my friends were listening to Wet Willie, Black Oak Arkansas, the Charlie Daniels Band, and Lynyrd Skynyrd. I could not bear that white trash, rock 'n' roll music. When Charlie Daniels later started singing that awful song about the Devil coming down to Georgia, I would just turn the dial on the radio.

My theory was that the hippie ideals I longed to embrace had been lost along the way as they filtered out from San Francisco. The only ideals that reached the Deep South were growing your hair long, dropping out, and smoking dope.

I was above all that.

My tastes in music were a little more eclectic. I loved vintage country-and-western music, and the swing music of the 1940s, especially the Andrews Sisters, Patty, Maxine, and Laverne. I loved

Dusty Springfield, especially her rendition of "Son of a Preacher Man," which is found on one of the best albums ever recorded, *Dusty in Memphis*. Miss Springfield brought her smoky voice over from England, sat down with a bunch of Memphis blues musicians, and the rest is vinyl history.

I also loved the music black people were listening to. I secretly tuned into WFLI—the Black Spot on Your Dial! I would sneak down to the Memorial Auditorium in downtown Chattanooga to hear Wilson Pickett sing "In the Midnight Hour," or Millie Jackson wail through "(If Loving You Is Wrong) I Don't Want to Be Right." Miss Jackson had an album that came out years later called *Get It Out'cha System*. I had to hide that album under my bed because the lyrics were so nasty. They were certainly not fitting song lyrics to be heard by a (very reluctant) Young Royal Ambassador for Christ.

I was the only white boy in the whole auditorium. They used to call me the Blue-Eyed Soul Brother! I could do all the dances, too. The white kids laughed at the way I danced during the prom, but in reality, I was way ahead of them.

I've always been a good dancer. In junior high school PE class, we were given a choice: play dodgeball or take ballroom dancing lessons. Hmm, let's see. Get creamed by a blood-red ball or whisk around the floor on my tippy-toes?

I was enthralled with ballroom dancing. The teacher was a German lady, Fräulein Something-or-Other, who tapped her stick in time to the music and barked orders as most of the kids stumbled around and around, stepping on each other's toes.

But not me.

Oh no, no. I was light as a feather. I swirled around, and even added a few kicks and twirls here and there. I had no idea what interpretive dancing was, but I loved making it up as I went along. My red-faced, sweaty partner had no choice but to keep up as best she could. Poor thing. I had her in a vise-like grip.

All of a sudden, the Fräulein banged her stick and jabbed me on the shoulder, mid-twirl.

"Mr. Jordan, may I remind you that the young lady is the picture. You, my dear, are but the *frame*."

Well, fuck that shit.

But those dancing lessons sowed the seeds. I loved keeping up with the latest dance crazes. There was this really cool black girl I went to school with named Blondell, who taught me a lot of my best moves. She used to call me "Itty-Bitty."

"There goes Itty-Bitty, the Blue-Eyed Soul Brother!"

One time, she saved my life.

As far back as I can remember, the student body at my high school had been known as the Brainerd High Rebels. When our football team ran onto the field, a mascot dressed as a Rebel soldier and mounted on a Tennessee walking horse paraded around the field, holding a Confederate flag. Our school fight song was "Dixie"!

"I wish I was in the land of cotton. Old times there are not forgotten. Look away! Look away! Look away! Dixie Land."

Well, there were a lot of people that thought the whole rigmarole was racist. So, in 1972, they tried to change the name to the Brainerd High Panthers, and race riots broke out. It even made the national news. I was caught in the middle because I had so many black friends, and that just wasn't done back then.

Blondell saw me walking down the hall one day. She called me to the side and whispered, "Itty-Bitty, you know I love you, but you better get your little white ass out of this part of the school. We're fixin' to rumble."

And with that, all hell broke loose.

Bricks started flying. Windows were broken. Students ran up and down the halls with bats. The National Guard was called in! A white boy from my church was dragged into a bathroom and beaten senseless, and hordes of rednecks in pickup trucks cruised the city looking for black people to kick the shit out of. I escaped through a window by the skin of my teeth—which, incidentally, has been the story of my life.

Years later, I was working as a host at the Hamburger Hamlet on Hollywood Boulevard, across from Grauman's Chinese Theatre. One night, as I counted out the register money, this very chic black girl came sauntering in the front door.

"Are y'all still open?" she asked in a Southern drawl.

"Yes, we are, Miss Blondell."

"Itty-Bitty!" she screamed. "The Blue-Eyed Soul Brother! Is it really you?"

We spent hours and hours catching up. She still knew all the best moves.

Gypsies, Tramps, and Queens

Here I am in Castle Leslie
With rows of books upon the shelves
Written by the Leslies
All about themselves.

attributed to Jonathan Swift

I ONCE stayed in a monastery built in the eighteenth century and rumored to have been used at one time as an insane asylum. It sat, like some great Victorian dowager, overlooking Lake Pantelimon on the outskirts of Bucharest, Romania. It had at some point been converted into a hotel called the Hotel Lebada. On the inside, the crumbling hotel looked like an overdone New Orleans whorehouse—with old marble, gold fixtures, and dusty, bloodred velvet drapes. I was shooting a low-budget independent horror movie called *Madhouse,* in what must have been the cells for the crazy people.

A tiny arm of land separated the hotel and lake from the Gypsy camps across the way. Gypsies, in this day and age? How exotic! The Romanian Gypsies still travel in brightly painted caravans pulled by pitifully skinny horses. They became my obsession, especially the dangerous-looking, long-haired men. But we had all been warned in no uncertain terms to stay away from the Gypsy camps.

We were shooting *Madhouse* in Romania as it was a whole lot cheaper than shooting in the States. I had been roped into this venture by my old friend Billy Butler, who had written the script and was also making his directorial debut. I was to play a nebbishy psychiatrist who gets his head chopped off. I had jumped at the chance. Years and years in sitcom hell had given me an insatiable hunger for film acting. All it took to get me on board for a feature film was two dollars a day and a hot meal.

Billy Butler and I had a history. Our friendship had survived all kinds of questionable behavior. One time we got into a drunken brawl after six very dirty martinis in a lovely French restaurant called La Poubelle. Back then, when I drank I was known as the Tiny Terror. I had a history of slapping people across the face. Sometimes, people whose faces I could barely reach.

Smack! "It's not always about you!"

Smack! "Well, honey, it ain't always about *you,* either!"

I must say, Billy certainly held his own in our little fracas. As I recall, we were thrown out into the street before we even had a chance to taste our escargots.

We had both ended up in desperate straits more times than I cared to remember. At our lowest point we were living in Koreatown with no electricity. But that is a whole other story. At the time of this rendezvous in Romania, each of us had cleaned up his act and gained a modicum of success.

My room at the Hotel Lebada had huge windows that opened out, overlooking the lake. I had packed my "location trunk," which consisted of all the necessities a homosexual must have at his disposal: a European feather bed, high-thread-count sheets, down pillows, and soft toilet paper. I raided the rambling, overgrown gardens that surrounded the hotel for fresh-cut flowers and befriended the maids, who gave me lovely old cut-glass vases to display them in.

I had also brought wonderful-smelling candles, which I burned at night while hanging out the window like a damsel in distress, staring at the moon and wondering what those Gypsy wastrels were up to across the way. I could hear their music and drunken laughter beckoning. And if I squinted up my eyes and leaned out, I thought I could see the colorful skirts of the women whipping about as they danced by a bonfire in the moonlight.

I could not help but wonder what it would be like getting frisky in the woods with one of those Gypsy boys. They were on every street corner in Bucharest, begging, scamming, and fortune-telling. What might those young Lotharios be willing to do for a few extra dollars?

Bucharest lay nearby like the Forbidden City.

It was recovering from its former communist regime, and danger still lurked around every corner. At night we were only allowed to go into the city with a car and driver, and we had at our disposal a fleet of ancient black Mercedes sedans with young, handsome, uniformed Romanian men to drive us about.

I was informed that the gay scene in Bucharest was very discreet. Homosexuality had been a punishable crime under the communist regime. We were told gay bars did indeed exist in Bucharest, but were warned to be careful in our quest to find them. It was all very wink-wink.

Being the most industrious of the gays in the crew, I set out to find a place where we could twist the night away among like-minded people. It took me a few weeks of nosing around, but I finally scored an address from a front desk clerk at another hotel, who batted his eyes and slipped me a hastily scribbled note. So that weekend a bunch of us piled into our chauffeured Mercedes sedans and took off, caravan-style, for the only gay bar in Bucharest.

When I was seventeen years old I decided that for my own sanity I needed to meet some queers. I

had heard that somewhere in downtown Chattanooga was a gay bar called the Cross Keys Lounge.
I called information with my heart beating frantically and got the address. It was down on Broad
Street near the infamous Cadillac Club, in a very
unseemly part of town.

I borrowed my mother's red Monte Carlo and
told her I was going to the public library one evening to do a research paper for school. Instead, I
sat across the street from the dubious establish-
ment for hours. I watched a few people go in and
out, lost my nerve, and drove home.

A week later I was back, sitting in the Monte
Carlo. This time, I gathered enough courage to
get out of the car and walk to the corner. I longed
to meet some queers! But once again, I chickened
out and went home.

On my third attempt, I got out of the car and
boldly strolled within a block of the front door. I
was standing there hoping against all hope no
one from my high school or church would drive
by. My goodness gracious, I was in the honor soci-
ety, was treasurer of the Spanish club, and had
just been elected junior class president. Plus, in
my church I was an active member of the Royal
Ambassadors for Christ. The news would have

spread like wildfire throughout the whole school and been whispered in every pew the following Sunday morning.

Scandalous!

While I was attempting to gather my courage to move toward the door, I saw something that will stay in my memory until the day I die. Two drag queens paraded down the street, arm in arm, in full regalia. I had no idea what a drag queen was, but I knew these two were men in dresses, makeup, and high wigs. Their feather boas whipped in the wind and they drunkenly teetered about on impossibly high stiletto-heeled shoes.

I stood frozen to the spot, both repulsed and deeply fascinated. They sailed closer and closer, looming before my eyes like the bow of an old pirate ship. One of the Creatures from the Hair Spray Lagoon stopped, cocked a hand on her hip, and eyed me up curiously from under at least three layers of false eyelashes.

"Well, I wish you'd look at this one, Miss Victoria. Idn't it precious? No bigger than a wore-out bar of soap. What are you doing out on these mean streets, little mister?"

I couldn't speak. I was so scared I thought I might start projectile vomiting.

"I think I know what this one is up to," said the other one with a knowing wink.

I wanted to take off running but I could not get my legs to operate properly. I felt weak and shaky all over.

"Oh yes, Sister Sue, I know that look." She leaned in toward me and whispered, "You're trying to gather up the courage to go in that big, bad, gay bar, aren't cha?"

"No I'm not!"

"You can't hide it from us, honey. We've all been there! Now come to Mama. Come on and help me, Sister Sue. We've got to be good Samaritans and get this scared, helpless creature into his first gay bar!"

And with that, they got on either side of me, grabbed my arms, and waltzed me down the street and through the doors of the Cross Keys Lounge. I suppose in everyone's life there is a defining moment, the moment when you realize that nothing will ever be the same again. For some it is standing at the altar with a beloved, saying "I do." For others it is watching the miraculous birth of a child, or receiving a diploma from some prestigious university.

Mine was the moment I stepped across the

threshold of the Cross Keys Lounge in downtown Chattanooga, Tennessee, in my junior year
of high school.

I think I exhaled for the first time in my life.

I was no longer alone.

And my God, it was loud! "Lola" by the Kinks
was blaring on the jukebox and I was struck by
the cacophony. All sorts of folks—from lawyers
in suits to men in dresses to butch women who
resembled Elvis impersonators—were crammed
into the tiny bar. The only thing they seemed to
have in common and to be celebrating wildly was
that they were all gay. Yippee!

I sometimes lament the diversification of the
gay community. It's wonderful that we're now
spread far and wide, straddling all socioeconomic
lines, color barriers, and age divisions. But today
young gay people not only have to find their tribe,
they must also find their tribe within the tribe.

Should one embrace the circuit party set? Or
the leather scene? How about the Log Cabin Re-
publicans? There's always the drag queen culture
or the Twinkie go-go boys. Like motorcycles?
How about Dykes on Bikes? Almost all major
cities now have gay choruses, and there's also a
whole gay culture surrounding live theatre. To be

or not to be an opera queen? For older queers there is even a gay senior citizens' center in Palm Springs, California, that has thousands of members. And if you're angry about the ways gays are treated, you can embrace activism and start rah-rahing with the Human Rights Campaign.

The choices are limitless. I've heard of a gay bar out in Venice, California, called the Rooster Fish that caters to young surfers. I once attended a gay roller-skating party in Grand Prairie, Texas, and saw young farm boys (who I thought could not possibly be gay) cavorting wildly around the rink holding hands and kissing. Some of them even had on silly skating skirts over their blue jeans and were skating backwards under the disco lights to the throbbing beat of the music.

We are not a glum lot, that's for sure. We are everywhere and it is just wonderful. But I still sometimes miss the feeling that I got in my first gay bar. It was the early 1970s and we were all bunched together, and there was a strong feeling of "us" and "them." We even confiscated the Pink Floyd song "Us and Them" as our anthem. It was on the jukebox and we played it over and over.

• • •

Back in Bucharest, we all piled out of our Mercedes and flooded into the only gay bar in town. Once again, I was struck with the feeling of "us" and "them." Romanians from all walks of life were crammed into the tiny space celebrating their gayness. Yippee!

It quickly became evident that somehow I had been chosen as the Belle of Bucharest. I was getting an enormous amount of attention. The young, good-looking American gay boys were being passed over in lieu of little old me. At one point I felt like a gay Hugh Hefner with seven silly blond Romanians giggling and crawling all over me.

It was as if I had won the lottery.

At first I thought maybe they knew me from television, but that was not the case. Apparently, most gay boys in Romania want a sugar daddy to get them out of the country. With my wandering blue eyes, gray hair, and chauffeur-driven car waiting outside, I must have had "American Sugar Daddy" written all over me.

Well, I am always one to take advantage of a winning situation.

All of a sudden, the door opened and in

walked the prettiest boy I have ever seen in my life. He was six feet tall and skinny as a rail, and he moved like a gazelle. He would have been right at home strutting the runway in Milan with his long flowing hair, piercing green eyes, and patrician-looking features. I swear I could not catch my breath.

He assessed the crowd and immediately took notice. He gave me a smile that pierced my heart, and then he winked at me. I almost fainted. I kid you not. It was like something out of a movie. I felt like a young Catherine Denueve.

It did not take this young man long to move in for the thrill. And off we went into the dark Bucharest night.

The next morning, as my young Adonis slept, I went downstairs for coffee and sweet rolls. I practically skipped along, whistling a merry tune. Suddenly, the head of hotel security loomed in my path, crooked his finger at me, and roughly paraded me into the hotel office.

I was told to sit, like a kid being reprimanded in the principal's office. He eyed me up and down. "I understand you have a young man in your room."

I could not believe what I was hearing. I told

him that I did indeed have a young man in my room and I huffily asked if there was a problem.

He said yes. The young man I had in my room was not a registered guest of the hotel.

I almost flew off the handle. I told him that this young man was *my* guest. I told him that the actress across the hall had her husband visiting for weeks and he was not a registered guest. Another actor had his manager staying with him and the manager was not registered. Why was I being singled out for having someone not registered staying overnight in my room?

I puffed up and asked him if this was a "gay" thing.

"No," he replied, "the problem has nothing to do with . . . that. The problem is that your young man looks . . . *Gypsy*."

The word hung in the air like a bad smell.

"Meaning?"

"Meaning, Gypsies are thieves. So I am telling you for your own good to watch your wallet, your passport, and anything else you do not want to turn up missing!"

I was aghast.

Against my better judgment I informed the head of security for the Hotel Lebada that the young man was a guest of mine and I trusted him implicitly and he would be spending a lot of time with me during my stay in Bucharest and we would both be down shortly to register him. What was I thinking? Had I lost my marbles? I barely knew this boy.

The head of security stared at me for a long time.

"I doubt he has any identification. Gypsies never do. If he is to remain on the premises he must have identification. We are expecting the Is-raeli junior soccer team next week and we are on high security alert. You must understand that this is all for your own protection as well."

When I informed my young man of the de-velopments, he was livid.

"I am *not* a Gypsy! Who says I am a Gypsy?" He stomped indignantly around the hotel room. His green eyes flashed and he kept throwing his long hair out of his face. I tried my best to calm him down.

"Julian, this all means nothing to me," I said, "but for you to stay you must be registered. Do you have any identification?"

He would not look at me, and spoke in the tiny voice of a child. "No. It was stolen. I need to take the train to my hometown of Sibiu to replace my identification."

"Then I'll send you to Sibiu. I will buy you a train ticket. This is really no big deal. Please calm down."

He barely acknowledged me. I could tell his feelings were still hurt, so I thought it best to leave him alone. I was expected shortly in the makeup room. We were shooting a scene outside in the gardens that involved mental patients kicking a soccer ball around. After I was made up and ready to go before the cameras, I stopped by the room to check on my young man.

"Julian?"

He was gone.

And so was my passport, cash totaling almost a thousand dollars, my leather bag, my wallet, my favorite Versace shirt, and all of my credit cards. I flew out of the room, down the stairs, and out into the garden screaming like a drunken banshee.

"That thieving Gypsy has wiped me out!"

As I sputtered and stomped about, Billy Butler pulled me aside, pinched my arm, and whispered violently, "Stop it right now and I mean it. The scene we are about to shoot is really important, and I don't need your drama."

"Billy, I was warned, but I didn't listen, and now my heart is broken. I can't possibly work!" I cried.

"Oh, cut the crap, Mary," Billy snorted. "You just met him last night! Now, get your gay ass over there in front of that camera before I smack you a good one like I did that night at La Poubelle."

I started to inform Billy that I would smack him right back, but I do not think my nerves could have stood another gay smackdown. I could tell that he meant business, so I acquiesced and we all went to work.

I was so wrapped up in the scene we were shooting I almost forgot about the terrible pickle I was in. At one point, Billy pulled me aside.

"He's behind the tree."

"What?"

"Your hustler is behind the tree."

"What are you talking about? What hustler?"

"The Gypsy who ripped you off is sitting over there behind that big tree."

I was stunned. I walked over and, sure enough, Julian sat cross-legged behind a tree. In his lap he held my leather bag, my wallet, and my Versace shirt. Nearby on the ground were my credit cards and money, neatly stacked.

"Julian?"

He looked up. There were tears streaming down his face. "I could not do it."

"But why would you? I was good to you."

"Because," he said, "it's all I know."

I sat beside him and stared out over the rambling, overgrown garden. He seemed genuinely remorseful. I could see the Gypsy camps off in the distance. What had I gotten myself into?

The next day, I sent him to his hometown on a train. He triumphantly returned with his identification and we presented it to the management at the hotel. The way they treated him was inexcusable. They would not look at him and when they did, they did so with disdain.

He was embraced, however, by the movie crew from America, and he blossomed under their attentions. He even cut his long, beautiful hair to look more presentable. While I worked all day getting my head chopped off and such, Julian played in the swimming pool. In the evenings, after a long siesta, we dressed for dinner. What an odd pair we made as we paraded into the finest restaurants in Bucharest. I bought Julian a new wardrobe at the Romanian Kmart. He seemed to favor the look of a 1980s rock star. I wanted to place emphasis upon his patrician looks and dress him up like a beautiful Brooks Brothers doll, but he liked things that were ripped up and held together with safety pins—a Romanian Rick Springfield.

There was always a moment as we walked into a fancy restaurant. People would notice us and everything would stop. Julian always defiantly stood his ground and proudly moved closer to me. I felt as if we were an interracial couple in the Deep South in the 1950s. These situations brought us closer and closer, and I began to feel incredibly protective toward him as well.

We stood united against the prejudice toward his Gypsy heritage.

Some crazy old broad I met in recovery once told me, "Honey, if you've got one foot in yesterday and one foot in tomorrow, you are in the perfect position to just shit all over today."

Julian truly lived in the moment, and it rubbed off on me. On my days off from shooting we took a delightful vacation to the Black Sea. We took the train to Constanta and checked into a beautiful hotel that spoke of the days of the Romanovs. We also rented a car and drove to Transylvania to see the hunting lodge of some king from days gone by and the castle of Count Dracula. It was magnificent. Surprisingly, Julian was an authority on the history of his country and loved regaling me with interesting tidbits.

The time for me to leave Romania came all too soon.

At the airport, he stood waving sadly as I walked away. In the car behind him was everything he owned, including his new rock star wardrobe carefully folded in a beautiful leather suitcase I had given him as a going-away present. He told me that he would treasure his new suitcase until the day he died. In the folds of the suitcase I had hidden a secret wad of cash he would find when he unpacked his clothes.

I think people who grow up with hard knocks learn to not expect much from life. So when life presents them with unanticipated treats, they are grateful but careful not to expect too much. I lived with this young man for five weeks, yet I knew nothing about his life. I had no idea where he came from, or where he went after he left me.

We got off to a rocky start, but he made up for

it. He gained my trust. He showed me his country and he tried to keep me safe and sound. He never once asked to be taken to America. He never once asked for any money for his services. Come to think of it, he asked for very little.

And he gave quite a lot.

Even though I gave him a cell phone with six months of free unlimited calling, I never heard from him again. I did not really expect to. I think we both knew there was nothing else to be said. But here's to my young man Julian wherever he may be—for putting a little gypsy in my soul.

Diva Crush

A high station in life is earned by the gallantry with which appalling experiences are survived with grace.

Tennessee Williams

Miss Faye Dunaway paid me the best compliment I have ever received. I was hired to do a few episodes of *It Had to Be You,* a situation comedy she was starring in with dear, sweet, beautiful Robert

Urich, who later tragically died of cancer. What a crush I had on Robert Urich! But we've been down that road before.

I was in awe of Faye Dunaway. I remember sitting alone in a darkened movie theatre in the throes of teenage angst, staring at her amazing cheekbones in *Bonnie and Clyde* (but lusting after Warren Beatty, of course). She was a legend.

The entire week of rehearsals she had been somewhat aloof, as she is very serious about her work and had many reservations about working in situation comedy. She wasn't available for chitchat, and any encounters up to that point had been strictly business. She had also been dressed very casually all week, with her hair pulled back and very little makeup. But after almost four hours in the makeup trailer, she paraded out in all her glory.

Faye Fucking Dunaway! She was bigger than life! And that is how a diva should be. Finally, we sat face-to-face in the greenroom, waiting to take our places onstage. Out of the blue, she leaned in and whispered in that smoky voice, "You remind me a lot of my dear friend Tennessee Williams."

I almost fell on the floor.

• • •

I think the biggest diva crush I've ever had was on Beverly D'Angelo. Having been a huge Patsy Cline fan my whole life, I thought Beverly's portrayal of Patsy Cline in *Coal Miner's Daughter* was breathtaking. I must have seen that movie a hundred times.

Years later, my friend Del Shores wrote and produced a movie called *Daddy's Dyin': Who's Got the Will?* with our manager, Bobbie Edrick. When I heard they had cast Beverly D'Angelo in one of the lead roles, I almost fainted. I plotted and planned how I could finagle my way onto the set to meet her. The movie was shooting in Drop, Texas. I kid you not. There's Dallas, and then as you head out of town there is Denton, then Ponder, then Krum, and then there is Drop. How in the hell was I going to get out to Drop, Texas?

Crawl on my hands and knees if I had to!

I had recently been in the enviable position of having been offered *two* television series in the same season. One was an offer to play a part on the second season of *ALF,* a hit series that starred a puppet from outer space. The other was a brand-new series, *The People Next Door,* starring Jeffrey Jones. At the time, Jeffrey Jones was enjoying huge success from his role as the principal in the blockbuster hit movie *Ferris Bueller's Day Off*.

My manager pooh-poohed the series offer from *ALF*.

"A series starring a puppet from outer space?" She laughed. "Oh, please, spare me! Plus, honey, you already kind of look like a little puppet from outer space."

Oh, well.

When the Jeffery Jones series was cancelled, I saw my opportunity to meet Beverly D'Angelo. I called Bobbie, who was already in Texas doing preproduction work on the movie, and told her I was so depressed I felt like jumping off a bridge. As I sniveled on, she grabbed at the bait.

"Well, honey, how about I fly you out here to godforsaken Drop, Texas, and we can hang out on the set. Would that cheer you up?"

"Yes, ma'am. Will I get to meet Beverly D'Angelo?"

"Of course, and you'll also get to meet Judge Reinhold and Beau Bridges and Keith Carradine and Tess Harper—remember her from *Tender Mercies*?—oh, and Sissy Spacek's going to be visiting because her husband Jack Fisk is directing!"

"Yeah, yeah, yeah . . . but will Beverly D'Angelo be around much?"

"She got in yesterday and she's a lovely girl, you two will really hit it off."

I screamed and locked myself in the bathroom.

When I got to Texas, the movie was shooting in an old ranch house out in the middle of nowhere. I stood around watching the rehearsal in the living room with my eyes glued to Beverly D'Angelo. She was really small. She has terrific boobs, a tiny waist, tons and tons of blond hair, and a real husky voice.

When we were introduced she was sweet, but she dismissed me immediately, as she was concentrating on the rehearsal. Not to be daunted, I spoke up and addressed the whole cast when they were on a break: "Listen, y'all, I'm driving into the Galleria in Dallas this afternoon if anyone needs anything."

Sure enough, Beverly came running over. "Sweetie, do you think you could buy me some panties? I packed so quickly I forgot my underwear. Can you believe it?"

She was digging in her bag for some money. I

was dumbfounded. I supposed she thought I was one of the production assistants for the movie. Why else would she ask someone she barely knew to buy her something so personal? I later learned that was just the way she was. Very free-spirited! I had almost forgotten that she was in *Hair* running around practically naked with a young Treat Williams.

I said, "I certainly don't mind buying you . . . panties. But I have to tell you I have no earthly idea what kind or size or anything about women's . . . panties."

"I'm easy to please. Size four and they have got to be cotton crotch. Wait a minute, come in here with me."

She paraded into the makeup room lugging her bag and I followed, sheepishly. She shut the door behind us and whispered as she continued to dig around in her enormous catchall, "I really wear a size six. I did *not* want any of the women overhearing my panty size. You know how women are."

"Size six," I replied.

"Cotton crotch," she repeated. "Don't forget that. Here's a hundred dollars. Just see what you can come up with."

I set off for Dallas like a man on a mission from God. In my hot little hand I held the crumpled hundred-dollar bill Beverly D'Angelo had given me. Scared to death I would forget, I whispered her instructions over and over on the drive to Dallas.

"Size six, cotton crotch. Size six, cotton crotch."

This was many years ago, before Victoria's Secret was so well known. When I saw the front of the store in the mall I thought, *Well,* this *looks like the place to buy panties for a movie star!*

The salesclerk was a rail-thin, impossibly chic older woman. She looked me up and down. She had on those half-moon reading glasses on a gold chain, and she peered over them like a whooping crane.

"May I help you?" She spoke like all those actresses from the 1940s.

I was so nervous my voice cracked. "Yes, ma'am. I'd like to buy some underpants . . . uh . . . for my wife."

"I see." She gave me a sly smile like she knew what was up. I swear she thought I was buying panties for myself! "Yes. Well, dear, what size panties does your . . . wife . . . wear?"

I blurted out my instructions. "Size six, cotton crotch."

"Well, dear, all our panties are cotton crotch. Follow me and I'll show you our vast selection."

She pulled out drawer after drawer. The selection was overwhelming. This was in the days before girls started wearing those little bitty butt-floss panties, but there were still some teeny-tiny pairs. I had no idea what kind of panties to buy for Beverly D'Angelo.

Miss Sand-in-Her-Vagina tried to steer me to some of the panties in bright, trashy colors, but I was raised in a home where four things were *always* white: bedsheets, bath towels, toilet paper, and paper towels for the kitchen. I naturally assumed that panties should always be white as well. I finally selected some nice panties—size six, cotton crotch, bikini cut—and called it a day. I was shocked that I could buy only four pairs with a hundred dollars, but I left the store swinging my bright pink shopping bag.

Mission complete.

On the way back I envisioned Beverly and me bonding over her new panties and becoming the best of friends. When I reached the set, she was still deep into rehearsal. I stood outside the crowd of crew members waving the Victoria's Secret bag, trying to get her attention.

She finally noticed me and waved a dismissive hand. "Put them over there with my things."

I was devastated. My feelings were so hurt. She didn't even say thank you! But I found out later from watching all the proceedings that when Beverly is working she is all business.

Beverly D'Angelo has a dear friend named Mela who travels with her everywhere. It was through Mela that Beverly and I finally bonded and became fast friends. I told Beverly all about my trip to Dallas and Miss Sand-in-Her-Vagina. We laughed and laughed.

Mela and I both used the laundromat down the street from the hotel as opposed to paying the exorbitant prices that the hotel charged for laundry. One time I noticed Mela loading the panties I had bought for Beverly into the washer.

"You do her laundry?" I asked, and pointed out the panties.

"Oh, those. Did you buy those for Beverly? You must have bought the wrong size. She gave them to me because they were waaaay too small."

That afternoon I cornered Beverly and told her if I ever got famous I had my Johnny Carson story ready. It was going to be about the time I bought panties for Beverly D'Angelo and she told me one size in front of everyone, then pulled me aside and told me a larger size, which I bought. But then even *those* turned out to be way too small for her fat ass.

"You know how women are about their panty sizes," I reminded her.

"You better not tell that story, and I mean it. I'll never speak to you again!"

Later on that day, Beverly pulled me aside. She was dead serious. "I've thought long and hard about your little panty story. I am giving you permission to use it, but listen—I want you to start at a size two. Then I pull you into the makeup room and tell you a size four. Then you buy a size four but they are just a little too snug. Got it? That's the story that goes on Carson."

Now, that is how a diva should be!

The Tears of the Israelites

Three things in human life are important. The first is to be kind. The second is to be kind. And the third is to be kind.

Henry James

I GREW up in a part of the country where the word "Jew" was often used as a verb. This is not something I am particularly proud of; it is just a fact. I heard the phrase "to Jew someone down" my entire life. I was in my early twenties galloping race horses at Belmont Park on Long Island before it was pointed out to me that this was highly offensive.

The thought had never crossed my mind.

I grew up in a religion that devoutly believed that the Jews had forsaken the Messiah and, sadly, all Jews were going to burn in an eternal lake of fire. I remember worrying myself sick about the poor Jews when I was a little kid. I also worried about the poor little children in Africa who had never even heard of Jesus. They were going to burn, too!

I remember that back in the 1970s there was a huge movement to get Jews to repent and accept Jesus as their personal Savior. It was called Jews for Jesus. Now, how silly is that? Judaism has been around a lot longer than Christianity. The Jews could have countered with their own movement. But I think the Jews were too smart to open that can of worms.

My friend Del Shores once told me a weird story. He knew a Jewish woman in Texas who answered her door one morning to find a neighbor lady standing there, anxiously wringing her hands.

"Honey, will you be my Jew?" she asked. "We're having 'Pack a Pew with a Jew' day at church. We're supposed to bring a Jew to church to sit in our pew and be saved and, hon, you're the only Jew I know."

The Jewish woman politely declined.

I don't remember knowing many Jewish people when I was growing up. The Jewish people in the South really kept to themselves in those days. In my public school the only way we knew who was Jewish was during an annual event called the DDT (Devoted Daughters of the Torah) Candy Sale. I remember we were always surprised at who was lugging around boxes of candy.

"I didn't know Debra Joy Goldstein was Jewish, did you?"

We grew up with so many misconceptions. One time someone told me the way you can recognize a Jewish woman is that she usually wears socks with her high-heel shoes. What was that about?

After the tragic death of my father, my mother had remarried, and we lived in an affluent area above Chattanooga called Missionary Ridge. There was a wealthy Jewish family in my neighborhood. The mother was a very powerful judge in the Chattanooga judicial system. And she rode a motorcycle to work.

You must understand that this was the early 1960s. We were barely out of the Eisenhower years. In those days, housewives rarely ventured out in anything other than housedresses. To see this grown woman in her daring pantsuit, straddling a motorcycle and flying down the road to work, was shocking.

It gave me the notion as a kid that Jews were a little wacky.

In 1969, I was fourteen years old and all I wanted out of life was to be a hippie. I felt so stuck in those Tennessee hills. It was just after the Summer of Love, the big hippie gathering in San Francisco, considered to be the birth of the movement (or, by many, the death). I'd gotten to know a lot of Jewish kids because they were more progressive than most of the kids in my town, and a lot of them already practiced the hippie ideals I was so desperate to embrace. The Jewish kids were the first hippies I knew. They all hung out at the bird sanctuary and smoked pot. I cannot tell you the crushes I had on those long-haired Jewish boys. You know Jesus was Jewish. And all those boys looked just like the pictures of Jesus we had on the walls at church. How sinful!

I read everything there was to read about the hippie movement. I devoured every word of *Slouching Towards Bethlehem,* Joan Didion's collection of essays about California during the 1960s. I especially loved the chapter about the Haight-Ashbury section of San Francisco. Back then I thought of San Francisco as Mecca. I wanted to run away and live there. I wanted to wear flowers in my hair! I grew my hair as long as my parents would let me and started locking myself in my bedroom, listening to the Grateful Dead.

My mother would yell, "What on earth is that racket?"

"Mom, it's the Grateful Dead!"

"Well, I'm grateful they're dead. Now, please cut it down!"

I read Jack Kerouac, too, with a vengeance. I would almost faint when there were slight suggestions that he might have been bisexual. He was so handsome. And if you read *On the Road* from the viewpoint of a little gay kid in Tennessee, it certainly sounded like Kerouac's autobiographical narrator had a huge crush on that other guy,

his idol Dean Moriarty, whose path he kept
crossing. And let's not forget that Jack Kerouac
lived off and on with his mother till the day he
died.

Sounds a little suspicious to me!

There were also rumors that Jim Morrison
was bisexual. What a looker he was! He was without a doubt the prettiest hippie to ever walk this
earth. I would pretend I was the only one who
truly understood Jim Morrison. I read all of his
poetry (which is basically just drug-induced babble). I pretended I knew what it all meant, even
the parts about the dead Indian lying on the road.
When Morrison was arrested for indecent expo-
sure, just the very thought of him pulling his
penis out of those tight leather pants onstage in
Miami made me almost collapse. Oh, what a crush
I had on Jim Morrison!

Many years later, in a trashy book about Andy
Warhol's Factory, there was a passage about Jim
Morrison at a party, lying on the floor completely
inebriated with his penis out, slowly playing
with himself. He supposedly passed out with his
flaccid member lying out of his zipper. This was
in the days before anyone had heard the term
"date rape," so all kinds of people gave him blow

jobs while he was passed out just to say they had sucked Jim Morrison's dick.

Thrilling!

Actually, it's kind of sad and definitely sick— but thrilling nonetheless! I wish I had been there, if only just to watch, of course.

I would sit for hours on end and daydream about Woodstock. I saw the documentary about nine times. I wanted so badly to be a part of all that was happening in California. I felt like the parade was passing me by. I find it interesting as a recovering addict and alcoholic that my idols back then were rock stars who are now all dead: Janis Joplin, Jimi Hendrix, and Jim Morrison.

It's funny how life turns out. When I did make it to San Francisco, I was in my late forties and sober for over five years. I had been invited to speak to a huge recovery group and was being flown up from Los Angeles. I was going to speak at the Bill Graham Auditorium. My mother mistakenly thought I was headlining the Billy Graham Crusade. She was ecstatic! Finally, I was doing something she could tell all her girlfriends in Sunday school about.

I love my mother.

She is always hoping for the best.

• • •

One Passover, my manager, Bobbie Edrick, invited me to celebrate at a seder with her family in Sherman Oaks. She also invited James Earl Jones; his lovely wife, Cee Cee (Cecilia Hart); and their son, Flynn. We all congregated at the home of Bobbie's uncle Aaron; his wife, Aunt Sarah; and Sarah's sister, Aunt Ruthie. The three of them were in their eighties but had gone all out to accommodate us. It was my first seder, so I was very excited.

Uncle Aaron was at the head of the table with Aunt Sarah on his right and Aunt Ruthie on his left. As Uncle Aaron read the part of "the reader," James Earl Jones responded with the part of "the participant." When James Earl Jones began to read, everything stopped. It sounded just like rolling summer thunder in the Deep South. "We shall now dip our fingers into the salt water to remind ourselves of the tears of the Israelites."

I looked around the Passover table and everyone was misty eyed. I got choked up and I'm not even Jewish. Something very special was unfolding. Can you imagine? James Earl Jones, reading ancient, sacred words from the Torah?

It was a precious moment that I will always remember.

Then it was time for someone to open the front door, in case the prophet Elijah should want to visit and bless the home—a wonderful Jewish tradition.

"Ruthie!" Uncle Aaron hollered, as Aunt Ruthie was a little hard of hearing. "Do you want to do the honors?"

"What?" Ruthie hollered back.

"Do you want to do the honors?"

"Of what?!"

"WILL YOU PLEASE OPEN THE DOOR FOR THE PROPHET ELIJAH?"

"All right, already. Quit yelling."

So Aunt Ruthie pulled herself up and took off toward the door. The conversation around the table continued until someone noticed the front door was open but Aunt Ruthie was nowhere to be found.

"Where is she?" wondered Aaron and Sarah.

"I hope she's not loose in Sherman Oaks," Bobbie said.

Everyone jumped up and headed for the door. Aunt Ruthie was standing on the porch.

"What are you doing out there, Ruthie?" asked Aunt Sarah.

"I don't know." Aunt Ruthie shrugged. "How should I know?"

"Well, come back in and eat," Uncle Aaron said. "We're at the part about the roasted egg."

What a feast it was! I'd never had food that tasted so good and was so lovingly prepared. Aunt Ruthie may have forgotten little things like why she was out on the porch, but she certainly had not forgotten how to cook.

Then came a portion of the ceremony where the youngest member at the seder was supposed to try and find the matzo cracker, which Uncle Aaron had hidden under his napkin during the dinner. Since James Earl Jones's son Flynn was the youngest person in attendance, he purloined the cracker when no one was looking.

"Who has taken the matzo?" asked Uncle Aaron, with fake astonishment.

The family gathered around Flynn and coached him to yell, "*I* have the matzo!"

"Oh, you do, do ya? Well, I tell you what, I am going to give you one dollar for that matzo cracker."

The whole family coached Flynn to yell back, "Not enough!"

And thus began a very funny bargaining process to try and get tightwad Uncle Aaron to part with more money.

"Oh, so you're gonna be a wiseacre, are ya? Okay, I'm gonna give you two dollars for the matzo."

"Oh, please," said some of the family members to Flynn, "the matzo is worth more than that. Tell him not enough."

"NOT ENOUGH!" yelled young Flynn, really getting into the spirit of the game.

When Uncle Aaron finally hollered, "Five dollars and not a nickel more," the family shrugged their shoulders and began to walk away.

"You need to take it, kid."

"He ain't going no higher, trust me on this one."

"Nope, kid, take the five."

When I was a little boy, my mother used to tell me that just because something popped into my head, it did not have to come out of my mouth. But I was enjoying myself so much, I piped up.

"No wonder Jews make good agents!"

Peter Gazing

To find someone here or there with whom you can feel there is understanding in spite of distances or thoughts unexpressed—that can make this life a garden.

Goethe

I HAVE always prided myself on being an astute judge of human nature. I am saddled with the constant desire to try and figure people out. To see what makes them tick.

When I was little, every summer my family would pile into our big station wagon and head to Florida. Sometimes it was Panama City, sometimes it was Jacksonville or Daytona Beach, but always, always Florida. Daddy would throw a twin mattress in the back for my twin sisters and me to loll around on.

The Redneck Riviera!

My favorite thing to do in Florida was walk up to the boardwalk in the early evening with my mother and "people-watch." We would sit for hours and watch all the people.

"Oh, look at these two," Mother would exclaim. "I bet they're up to no good. Look at the way she's dressed. I cannot believe she goes out in public like that! And he looks like someone you'd see on the post office wall in a mug shot."

"I guess some people don't care if they look trashy," I'd cluck, wise beyond my years. "Trashy" was my new favorite word. It was right up there with "tacky" and "common."

"What do you think's going on with that couple over there?" my mother would ask. "Why on earth would a woman that pretty be with someone so ugly? Low self-esteem, I suppose. Or maybe at one time he was a looker. But he sure has let himself go. Probably drinks."

"Maybe she still loves him. She remembers when he was young and handsome," I would pipe in, always the romantic.

Those were some fun times!

Now, Billy Bob Thornton is a conundrum that sparks the imagination. There is something about him that makes me want to study him, like a bug on a pin. In the early 1990s Billy Bob and I worked for several years on the situation comedy series *Hearts Afire*. The show also starred John Ritter, Markie Post, and Conchata Ferrell.

I could not figure Billy Bob out to save my soul. And bear in mind, this was years before *Sling Blade* catapulted him into stardom. He was just a working actor back then. He had written, produced, and starred in one feature film that had given him a little notoriety, but he certainly was not the household name he is today. But there was something intriguing about him.

One night, John Ritter, my twin sisters, and I were sitting in a booth at Jerry's Famous Deli after the show, and John went off on this diatribe about Billy Bob's phobias. It was hair-raising—

something about not being able to eat around a black-and-white TV and some big fear of antique furniture.

John wanted me to hear about it straight from Billy Bob. He was always putting me up to something. John implored me, "You have got to find a way to get him talking. Once you get him started, he'll go on and on. It's really amazing. I can't do it justice."

"But how can I get him talking? If I walk up and just ask him about his phobias, won't he think you put me up to it?"

"Tell him that you are riddled with phobias. And then ask him if he has any," John suggested.

"What if he asks me to talk about my phobias first?" I countered.

"Then just make some up. Tell him you're scared of spiders crawling out of the toilet. You have got to get him to talk about it. It's mind blowing. It's like nothing I've ever heard."

But no matter how many times I tried to broach the subject with Billy Bob, I would chicken out. I don't know why. It just seemed too personal. It was like asking him about his masturbation habits. Or how many bowel movements he had

each day. But after what John had told me, my
fascination with Billy Bob grew even more. I
couldn't keep my eyes off him.

Finally, I struck pay dirt. There was this one
time Billy Bob somehow got stuck in Phoenix,
Arizona, and would not fly home. Refused! He
was deathly afraid of flying.

So we all sat around and waited while the
higher-ups figured out how to get Billy Bob home
in time for the shoot. I think they ended up sending a limo to bring him all the way from Phoenix.
But that was part of Billy Bob's charm. People
were always willing to do things for him. Why,
I'm not sure. There was something sweet and
childlike about him. Something about Billy Bob
made you want to pat him on the back and assure
him that it was all going to work out.

Once we were shooting an episode where my
character, Lonnie Garr—a forty-year-old virgin
who lived with his overbearing mother, who was
always making him go bra shopping at Sears—is
allowed, after much coercion, to join the all-male
club in town.

There was a scene where my character skips
into the bathroom the night of his induction into
the club, sidles up to the urinal between John's

character and Billy Bob's, and announces, "I feel like Cinderella at the ball."

Billy Bob's character, a weary Vietnam vet turned journalist, was supposed to move down a few urinals and say, "I don't pee next to men who say they feel like Cinderella. It's just this rule I have."

On the night of the shoot, Billy Bob, John Ritter, and I were standing at the fake urinals waiting for the lighting guys to light the scene. Billy Bob started doing this funny thing where he would stand close to the urinal, pretend to pull his penis out, and then thump the bottom of the urinal with his fingers. From the back, it looked like whatever Billy Bob was pulling out of his pants was so huge that it banged against the bottom of the urinal.

Hilarious!

He was getting huge laughs, so he did it again and again. Finally, the director came over and told him to stop doing it because the sound was being picked up. At that point, several of the actors who worked on the sitcom on the soundstage next door snuck in as a practical joke and took their places at the urinals. So when the director called "Action!" again, all kinds of shenanigans ensued. Put straight guys at a row of urinals and that's what you get.

Right in the middle of the mêlée, John Ritter leaned over to me and whispered, "If Billy Bob really pulled it out, you'd fall in love."

Now, please understand, there was not a gay bone in John Ritter's body. Trust me. But he was the kind of guy who was so comfortable with his sexuality that gay men did not inhibit him in any way. That is what I loved about him. He was so gay friendly. And I must say I miss him desperately. I have always judged famous people by the way they treat my family. When my mother and twin sisters came to the set of *Hearts Afire,* John made the biggest fuss over them.

When John died, I was so honored to be asked to attend his memorial service. Everybody in Hollywood was there. When the entire USC marching band charged down the aisle and played John on to greener pastures, there was not a dry eye in the house. John Ritter was a national treasure and I miss him. I especially miss the way he used to tease me.

This brings us back to Billy Bob's pecker.

I was taken aback. "What do you mean?"

"It's really big," John said.

"How do you know?"

"We went surfing at his house in Malibu and I saw it."

I did not know whether to believe him or not. I could see the twinkle in his eye and I knew he was up to something. My eyes must have been big as saucers and my mouth was hanging open. John could not believe the response he was getting.

"How big is it?" I implored.

"I don't remember exactly."

"They why did you tell me I'd fall in love?"

"I was joking."

"John, do not joke about these things. You cannot do this to a gay man. This is really important stuff."

"Okay, okay, it was huge. It hung down like a *rope*."

I almost hyperventilated. I thought I was going to pass out right there in front of the studio audience.

There is an old joke around the gay community that goes like this: There are two things I hate: a size queen and a tiny dick.

I do not want to go into all the ins and outs of being a size queen, but I will say that I have always been fascinated with large members. One time when I was in jail (more about that later), I had to shower with this big, nasty redneck who immediately warned me that he knew "what" I was and "there better not be any peter gazing!"

Guilty!

I've been up to that since I was a kid. It all began at church camp. I would make all kinds of excuses to sneak into the communal shower room. I would position myself at the mirror so that I could see backwards into the showers. Then I would pretend to wash my hands, comb my hair, brush my teeth, clean out my ears, trim my nose hairs, pluck my eyebrows, read my Bible—anything I could think of. I wanted to see the older boys lather up. They already had pubic hair! It was captivating beyond belief. I kept a mental register of who was hung and who wasn't.

It changed my whole perspective on life. Everything became "Does he have a big one or not?" *How about that boy over there? He probably has a little tiny one. Or how about this one coming along? I bet he has a big, fat one.* It has kept boredom at bay for years. And I am still at it.

No one is safe from my scrutiny.

Not construction workers, policemen, lawyers, weathermen on TV, school principals, coaches, NASCAR drivers, four-star generals, other military men, a U.S. president or two (excluding Bush Jr.—*never thought about it could care less*), English heirs to the throne, all male movie stars except Tom Cruise (whose religious fervor bugs me), mayors (especially ones from San Francisco), and certainly no man who dares to venture out in those tight bicycle shorts.

They are really asking for it!

A straight friend once complained to me about how gay men sometimes followed him into the locker room at the gym. He said they would stand around pretending to do things so as to watch him undress. I told him he ought to be flattered. He said it made him nervous. I told him maybe that was how most women felt when men undressed them with their eyes. How about them apples?

While he was contemplating that, I threw this at him: If there was a way that, without causing too much of a ruckus, he could wander into the ladies' dressing room just to observe, would he do it? He told me, "With so much snatch running around the gym, I probably wouldn't even be able to work out, I'd be wandering in and out!"

Touché! What's good for the goose is good for the . . . gay goose.

Or whatever.

One time I was hired to do a guest spot on the television show *Lois & Clark*, starring Dean Cain and Teri Hatcher. I played Resplendent Man, a fey little superhero who steals Superman's powers. I had to wear tights! I was twenty pounds heavier than I am now, and this was before I got sober, so I was bloated from all the alcohol. I looked like a beach ball with arms. I was sent over to the Warner Brothers wardrobe department to be fitted into purple-and-orange tights. I had to stand in front of a three-way mirror as the wardrobe people all gazed upon my fat ass.

One of the ladies casually looked right at my crotch and said, "Do you think he'll need what Dean needs?"

At least that's what I thought she said. Did I hear her correctly? What did Dean need? I could not get her casual comment out of my mind. Was he so tiny "down there" they padded him?

I doubted that.

It had to be the other way around. Maybe he was so big "down there" that the outline of his penis showed, and they were afraid it looked obscene. Maybe they had to construct a special garment to keep everything in line and looking like a well-hung Ken doll, so the network wouldn't get letters.

My mind began to wander. And wonder.

The first day of work, I showed up on the set determined not to "peter-gaze," or at least not to get caught at it. I had to remain diligent. Dean Cain was no dummy—I had heard he was a Princeton graduate. When they introduced us, I kept my eyes on the ceiling. I looked up for so long I almost lost my balance. As I recall, he even glanced up to see what I was looking at.

Dean Cain was stunning, and the sight of him strutting about in his Superman outfit was truly magnificent. Because his outfit was polyester and did not "breathe," he had a habit of taking his arms out of his Superman suit, rolling it down, and sitting in his chair shirtless, like surfer boys do with their wetsuits. It was the only way he could cool off between takes.

All I have to say is this: Thank you, dear Lord, for nonbreathable polyester.

I could not take my eyes off of him. He had that really lean, swimmer's build. And he was not at all self-conscious about his God-given looks. In fact, he was totally unaware of the little fat queer in his purple-and-orange tights desperately trying to keep his wits about him. *I will not peter gaze . . . I will not peter gaze . . .*

It was torture, pure and simple.

But I must admit, I peeked. Just several on-the-sly peeks. And I don't think I got caught. I always picked the times he was fussing about Teri Hatcher. There was definitely something going on "down there," and I do not believe Dean Cain "needed" anything. But . . . that is all I'm going to say on the subject.

Over the next year of filming *Hearts Afire,* Billy Bob and I became really good friends. I mean, I was never invited to his house in Malibu to surf, but we would hang out on the set. We have the exact same sense of humor. And Lord knows, we are both about two generations away from government cheese. Not exactly poor white trash but it's in both our gene pools somewhere back there.

I gave Billy Bob one of the best presents he ever received. I had somehow gotten ahold of this videotape of a televangelist from Dallas, Texas, who had some minor tics. Someone within his ministry had taken portions of his sermons and added fart noises. The preacher would holler "Jeeeeesus!" and his head would jerk in a slight tic—and then a real loud fart noise would thunder forth. Or he'd yell "O Lord, I sense thy presence!" and a long, slow one would venture out. I gave this tape to Billy Bob for Christmas. I have never seen anyone laugh that hard in my whole life. At one point, he lay on the floor holding his sides, begging me to stop the tape. I would put the tape on "pause" until Billy Bob caught his breath, and then I'd hit "play" and he'd guffaw and carry on like the town drunk.

But through it all, I could not get the size of his wiener off my mind. He'd be going on about something or another and all I could think was, *I wonder if we're talking girth as well as length?* Or he'd be telling me a funny story about a man in his hometown they called "the fart sniffer" and all I could think was, *Cut or uncut?*

It was a terrible obsession.

When *Hearts Afire* was cancelled right out from under us, I was sad beyond belief. All I could think about was Billy Bob marching off into the sunset with his big penis. I'd probably never see him again for a really long time.

And I didn't.

Years later, I picked a visiting cousin of mine up at the airport. She immediately informed me that all she wanted to do was see movie stars. I told her I knew a few places where we might go, but first I wanted to take her to a restaurant near Malibu called Gladstone's. It sits right on the ocean and has a real California feel to it. As we stepped out of the car and into a beautiful Pacific Ocean breeze, I heard an old, familiar voice.

"And then, there's Leslie Jordan. . . . He's a character if there ever was one."

It was Billy Bob! My cousin's mouth fell open. My mouth fell open. He looked so good! Thin, but very healthy and vibrant. There was a new-found calmness and serenity that I did not remember. He had his two sons with him; they were now practically teenagers. We exchanged pleasantries, but all I could think about was his big dick. And with my sweet cousin standing right there beside me!

I almost gathered up the courage to ask Billy Bob for a peek. Just so I could put it to rest. It had been been on my mind for years and years.

Why deny me that? But I knew it was not meant to be. There are probably a lot of things I'll go through life without seeing—the *Mona Lisa,* the Taj Mahal, the pyramids. And I'll probably never see Billy Bob's wiener, either.

Matt Lauer

Well, well, well, Karen Walker. I thought I smelled gin and regret.

Beverley Leslie, *Will & Grace*

I suppose fans of *Will & Grace* might assume that the role of Beverley Leslie was written for me. Not true. Believe it or not, the part was written for Joan Collins. As the story goes, Miss Collins was supposed to steal the maid, Rosario, away from the character Karen Walker, played by Megan Mullally—thus leading to a *Dynasty*–like catfight over a billiard table. Each actress was supposed to pull the other's wig off. Apparently Miss Collins had backed out of the role.

Who knows why? Who cares? It was certainly advantageous to Mr. Leslie Jordan. That's all that really matters.

I was told by my agent to put on the adorable

white suit that John Ritter had given me when I worked with him on *Hearts Afire* and trot over to the *Will & Grace* production offices. The producers wanted a Truman Capote type. I walked in wearing my white suit and chattering away like castanets.

The producers took one look and said, "You're it!"

I did one episode. This led to another, then to another. And all of a sudden, I was family. I became a real part of the show. When I won the Emmy, I was so honored. I have always felt that there are two ways to combat homophobia. One is through humor. I learned that during dodgeball in junior high school. Some redneck would holler "Smear the queer!" and I'd have to tap-dance or get creamed. And the second way to combat homophobia is to "put a face on it." America welcomed these characters into their homes. We laughed. We loved. And progress was made. I was privileged to be a small part of that.

In the many years I worked on *Will & Grace,* I cannot remember a guest star I was more excited about than Matt Lauer. I was not around for Elton John, Madonna, or Cher. But not even Jennifer Lopez or Matt Damon excited me like Matt

Lauer. (I do remember a slight crush on Seth Green. I remember wishing he had an overbearing mother and a weak father. We would make an adorable couple.) But Matt Lauer still won, hands down. When I first saw him, I got weak in the knees. The first thing you notice about Matt Lauer is how skinny he is. Skinny and tall as a Georgia pine.

Matt Lauer is also handsome, in a very unconventional way. You cannot take your eyes off of him. He's got it in spades. Every time he came around, all I could do was giggle like a shy Japanese girl behind her fan. It was ridiculous. He introduced himself and I just giggled and simpered with my hand over my mouth.

I thought, *Get a grip!* But when I tried to talk, my voice held a fairy-tale quiver. He must have thought I was retarded. Or maybe he thought I was slightly autistic.

He finally put me at ease with his talents as a good interviewer. He asked a couple of questions about me and that was all it took. We actors love to wax poetic about our favorite subject—ourselves!

We were shooting one of the "live" episodes,

which require a lot of rehearsing. There is no margin for error, so we did each scene over and over again. In one scene, Will (Eric McCormack), is at a party at the mansion of Karen Walker (Megan Mullally), and through a series of events ends up in the bathroom without his pants on.

Will storms out of the bathroom clad only in his underwear and immediately pops back in and sheepishly says, "In case anyone's wondering, Beverley Leslie comes up to my penis."

Then Grace (Debra Messing) was supposed to deliver the zinger: "Oh, so you just tea-bagged a dwarf!"

Well, there was much discussion as to whether that would get past the censors. And sure enough, the notes came in: " 'Tea bag' can be used as a noun! It *cannot* be used as a verb! Period. End of discussion."

We were all standing around tossing out alternate lines when Matt Lauer leaned in to me and asked, "Is that really a popular term with the general public?"

I thought he did not know what "tea-bagging" meant. So I said, "Well, it's where you put your balls in someone's mouth and go up and down."

"I know what the term means!" he spouted. "What I'm wondering is, how many people out in TV land would even get the joke?"

I could have died on the spot. I was mortified. Oh, how I wished for the floor to just open up and swallow me! I would go down in infamy as the dummy who tried to teach Matt Lauer what "tea-bagging" meant. What if I ever got famous enough to be on the *Today* show? They'd never let me on!

"Good Lord, no, we can't have Leslie Jordan on the show," they'd say. "He has a terrible potty mouth."

But let me tell you something about Matt Lauer. He has a great sense of humor and is perfectly willing to make fun of himself. He rolls with the punches. And that's what makes him good at what he does. The whole tea bag joke was replaced with a joke insinuating that Matt Lauer sits down when he pees! Now that is a good sport. A manly man like that, letting people think he sits down when he pees.

I doubt he even remembers our conversation. I hope not. Because I still have a huge crush on Matt Lauer. When I see him on that morning show, all I can do is giggle.

When You Swish upon a Star

I celebrate myself, and sing myself.
Walt Whitman, *Song of Myself*

IF YOU had asked me in 1997, the year I finally got sober, if I was a proud, openly gay man, I would have replied, "Honey, I've ridden floats half naked right down the middle of Santa Monica Boulevard!"

But when my medicine was taken away, the oddest thing happened. At forty-two years of age, I found myself completely riddled with internal homophobia. I had first started drinking and using drugs when I was fourteen years old and that was the same time I was coming to the realization I was gay. I found out pretty quickly it was a lot easier to deal with being gay when I was high. So I just stayed high (or sort of high) for about thirty years! Was there a problem with that?

One of my counselors in rehab was a real funny Mexican queen. He told me, "Girl, you are a fag-hating fag. Do you realize that?"

I replied, "I don't hate fags. I only hate really effeminate fags."

The counselor looked me up and down. "Hello!"

When, consciously or unconsciously, we recognize the things we hate about ourselves in others, that is when the finger pointing starts. I hated being a sissy. I have been a big sissy all my life. I was consumed with self-loathing. And who could blame me? What is the worst thing a kid can call another kid?

"Fag!" "Queer!" "Pussy boy!"

All my life, I have been told that I am self-absorbed. I can remember my mother telling me, even when I was little, "Honey, it is not always about *you*." And every single time I have attempted any kind of long-term relationship, the person has walked out the door with those same words.

But I never believed that. I thought that to be self-absorbed you had to think highly of yourself. I thought only conceited people who loved staring at their reflection in the mirror were self-involved. Wrong. The most self-absorbed people are actually consumed with self-loathing. They really cannot see beyond their internal hatred, and it becomes all about them.

My journey into sobriety has been an amazing journey into my Queerdom. I realize now that my own homophobia had caused my self-loathing. There is a line in Del Shores's play *Southern Baptist Sissies* that is an achingly accurate portrait of growing up gay in the Baptist church. One of the characters looks around the church where he was raised and says, "This is where we learned to hate ourselves." It really struck a chord with me.

I now consider my "coming out" period to be the first ten years of my new sober life. Even though I had been living as an "out" gay man for over twenty-three years, it was all in an alcohol- and drug-induced fog.

My rehab counselor made an astute judgment. He told me that it seemed from listening to my story that my greatest fear was of groups of heterosexual men.

"No shit," I replied. "It wasn't exactly a picnic on the playground!"

He strongly suggested that I join an all-male, or stag, recovery group. He told me that gay men have no idea how to socialize. All we know how to do is sexualize. The thought of walking into a room full of heterosexual men—especially a room where you're supposed to share your innermost secrets—made my stomach do triple backflips.

But at the time, thank goodness, I was desperate enough to do as I was told. I joined a stag recovery group. At the first meeting I sat in my chair, trying not to shake like a little Chihuahua. I was that scared. It didn't help matters that I had forgotten to leave my precious "murse" in the car. A murse is a man purse. Plenty of straight boys carry bags, but it is the way the bag is carried that makes it a murse.

The room smelled of testosterone. Caveman testosterone. I felt so left out. I felt there was something going on that I have never been able to feel a part of, something that seems to come so easily to heterosexual men. It's that back-slapping, loud-crowing, boot-thumping, crotch-grabbing, spitting-on-the-floor brand of masculinity that has always escaped me. We went around the room introducing ourselves and I fell into the old trick of trying to lower my voice.

It was useless.

I could tell that they were on to me. Near the end of the meeting, the leader called on me to share. I thought I was going to shit my pants. To make matters worse, I had to get up and walk to a podium. I tried not to walk like Bette Midler in concert. I was very self-conscious, trying not to swish. But as I stood there facing the enemy, something cathartic happened. I instinctively knew this was the jumping-off point. It was like when I had finally gotten up the nerve to mount the ladder to the high-diving board. I remember looking down knowing I had to jump. There was no way I was going to make all those kids behind me go back down the ladder to let me down.

It was sink or swim.

I took a deep breath. "My name is Leslie and I am an alcoholic and a drug addict. But more importantly tonight, at least for me and my recovery, I need to say this out loud: I am a homosexual."

I paused. I was waiting for one of those guys to snicker and shout "No shit!" But nothing happened. The room was deathly quiet.

"And I am scared to death of you guys," I continued nervously. "I am scared that you will be disgusted by me. I am scared that you will laugh at me behind my back. And I am real scared that you will shun me. But I am here tonight because of my sobriety. I was given direction to join this group and I am too scared right now to not take direction. I guess this is what you call a surrender."

For the first time in my life, I told the truth.

I was swamped after the meeting. The unconditional love in that room was overwhelming. That night, I became a part of something very important. I never missed a meeting for years and years. It's not as if we all went out together and bird-dogged chicks, but I became an integral part of that group.

I had always thought heterosexual men were fearless and shameless. I learned from the group that heterosexual men are more fear- and shame-ridden than any gay man I have ever met. I don't think little boys are raised right. We are raised to not show our fear. We are raised to be the protector, and not to be protected. The emotional landscape of most men is a minefield of fear and shame.

When I heard some of these huge, butch men take the podium and talk, some with tears streaming down their faces, it was so poignant, I often forgot to breathe. A couple of times I realized I was not breathing and almost toppled over.

Oh, great, I thought. *What would they think if I fainted out of my chair still clutching my murse?*

One of the men in that group suggested I carry a card he gave me. It read: WHAT YOU THINK OF ME IS NONE OF MY BUSINESS.

I carried that card in my wallet until it fell apart, and by that time I no longer needed it.

I remember when I was six years old, I walked out of Sunday school and told my daddy that I was never, ever going back. I stomped my foot to get my point across, as I was already a little fledgling drama queen.

"Oh, son, what are you talking about? You love Sunday school. You love Mrs. Townsend and all the Bible stories and games."

"But, Daddy, they laugh at me."

My dad got down on one knee and patiently explained to me, man to man, the difference between laughing "at me" and laughing "with me." He told me that I had been given a gift from God, and that was the ability to make people laugh. What an amazing gift! My dad then told me a Bible story about someone hiding his light under a bushel. He made me promise that I would never hide my light, that I would always let it shine.

I learned to be myself in front of those straight men. I learned that there is no big shame in being somewhat effeminate. I learned that people are drawn to others who are comfortable in their own skin—that the most off-putting people are the ones who try to pretend that they are something other than what they really are.

I learned to let my light shine.

But most important, those men taught me what it means to be a man. They picked up where my dad had left off, when he was snatched away from me when I was just eleven. It was as if I had been in a holding pattern since his death, just waiting for someone to take up the slack. I became their eager apprentice. I learned that being a man has very little to do with how far you can throw a football, how much weight you can lift, or how many women you've bedded—all those things that I am such a failure at. It matters not one iota that I never learned to walk and to talk like a man. Those men taught me that a man just has to have a code to live by. And they helped me find that code.

As long as I remain true to my own code, I am a man.

Luke Perry

A fair slim boy not made for this world's pain,
With hair of gold thick clustering round his ears. . . .
Oscar Wilde

LUKE PERRY broke my heart. I know this is getting ridiculous. I know it sounds like I am love-struck and boy crazy, but he really did. Before he became famous as Dylan McKay on *Beverly Hills 90210,* he lived across the street from me for two years. This was during the time I was living in the bad part of Hollywood and cavorting with a seedy cowboy. Luke warned me constantly about the company I was keeping, but I did not listen. I would not listen to anyone.

"I got a bad feeling about that boy," Luke would tell me. "He's got a teardrop tattoo below his eye. Do you know what that means?"

"No. And I don't want to know. I'm having

enough problems concealing the awful swastika tattoo he has on his hand."

Luke and his friend David lived together in straight-boy squalor. I had huge schoolgirl crushes on both of them. As a neighborly gesture, I sent my long-suffering maid Irma over to clean on Saturday mornings. She came back with horror stories in broken English of filth involving David's dog, Sasha, and Luke's potbellied pig, Jerry Lee. Let's just say that both David and Luke existed happily in conditions that would have driven a gay man to desperate measures.

One time they were trying to arrange their Salvation Army furniture in the best possible configuration for beer drinking and TV viewing. They asked my advice, since gay men are supposed to know about these things.

"Leslie, if this was your living room, what would you do?"

"Kill myself," I said, and swished out the door.

Right at that time, Luke landed the pilot of *Beverly Hills 90210* and I landed the pilot of *Top of the Heap*. We were both ecstatic, as he had been laying concrete to pay the bills and I had a cowboy with a very expensive drug habit to support. Both shows were on the Fox network, which at the time was fairly new. We had high hopes.

Luke's series made television history, while mine bit the dust after six episodes.

Luke Perry became famous almost overnight. It happened for him so fast it was mind-boggling. One day he was laying concrete and within a few months he was a household name. I walked into the grocery store and there was Luke Perry on the cover of *People, Vanity Fair,* and every *Teen Beat* magazine on the rack.

I looked out of my window once and there was a news van parked in front of Luke's house— and there was Maria Shriver, long before she married Arnold What's-His-Name. She was standing in the dirt yard, checking her makeup with a handheld mirror. I was so embarrassed. I tried to send Irma over to at least clean up after the pig, but she refused. I suppose Irma had her limits. Luke was oblivious. He and Maria Shriver paraded up and down the street chatting away, followed by a cameraman.

After the story aired, some really ambitious teenagers must have spotted a street sign, because suddenly we were besieged with young girls desperate to catch a glimpse of Dylan from *90210!*

They would drive up and down the street at all hours of the day and night. I got fed up with the whole scene and started chasing the hormone-crazed teenagers away, shouting obscenities.

One time, the Fox network was hosting some sort of charity softball game and the publicity department asked all the actors on the Fox TV shows to participate. I certainly cannot play softball, because I throw like a girl, but I had an ulterior motive in participating. I had a little speech planned in case any roaming news unit stuck a camera in my face.

"Hey, everybody! I'm Leslie Jordan from Fox's new show, *Top of the Heap*. I'd like to tell all those mean boys in Chattanooga, Tennessee, who tortured me during dodgeball to kiss my very rich TV-star ass!"

My big moment never came. I sat on the bench the whole time and was completely ignored. Luke and his new buddy Jason Priestly arrived in a brand-new white Mercedes, and the TV crews went ballistic. It was like those two were the Beatles. It took hordes of security guards to keep the screaming girls at bay. I was worried that someone would get hurt, as all the teenage girls had their perky little breasts mashed against the fence.

At one point Luke and Jason lit cigars. Why they were smoking cigars during a softball game was a mystery to me—must be a straight-boy thing.

But one little girl who could not have been more than twelve yelled, "Hey, Luke! I'll smoke your cigar!" And then she licked her lips! I wanted to march over there and wash her little garbage mouth out with soap.

Eventually, David moved out and Luke lived in his little house all alone. He spent a lot of time in his bedroom with the drapes closed. I was worried about him, but I soon realized he just needed a break from the insanity of his new life. He told me he really needed a place to call his own, and to please not give Irma a key. It was important to him. I asked how she was going to get in his house to clean up, because I knew Luke liked to sleep in on Saturdays, and he asked if I would come over and let her in. Well, my goodness gracious, that meant that I had to get out of bed on Saturday morning at an ungodly hour, traipse across the street, and let *my* maid in!

But since I was lovestruck and boy crazy, I did just that. Sometimes Irma would come waddling back over to my house, wake me up, and complain that Luke would not let her into his room to retrieve the dirty laundry. So I'd schlep back across the street in my pajamas and bang on Luke's door. I suppose it made it all worthwhile to be able to see Luke Perry, the young heartthrob of America, tangled up in his bedsheets half asleep! I would stand and stare longingly as if he were a Botticelli painting.

Even though I was cavorting with murdering trash straight from hell myself, I was worried about the company Luke was keeping. I was like Gladys Kravitz on *Bewitched*. I would sit for hours and hours peeking out my curtains, observing the goings-on across the street. I saw Luke hopping in and out of limousines at all hours of the night with Alexis Arquette (youngest brother to Rosanna, Patricia, and David), who was then performing drag under the name Eva Destruction. I knew there was not a gay bone in Luke's body, but who knows what the tabloids could cook up?

I worried myself sick. I thought it might end his career. Luke didn't seem to care. When I broached the subject, he told me that Alexis was a good friend and he did not give a shit what people thought. In retrospect, I realize I was insanely jealous of their friendship. It is a minor miracle

I did not borrow my cowboy's crossbow when I was high and shoot that damn drag queen dead in her tracks.

And then one day Luke was gone. Gone! The house across the street sat completely deserted. He had moved out in the dead of night. I called his cell phone but it had been disconnected. I was beside myself. At the time, Luke's assistant was Amanda Anka, daughter of the singer Paul Anka. When Paul wrote his smash-hit single "Having My Baby," Amanda was the baby he was singing about! She is now married to Jason Bateman. Anyway, Amanda told me that Luke had bought a house out in Tarzana. I asked for his new phone number.

"Leslie, I promised him I wouldn't give it to anyone."

"Amanda, come on. He is my friend. I fed him Thanksgiving dinner two years in a row when he couldn't fly home. I shared my maid with him! I'm not some obsessed fan."

I was almost in tears. I felt so abandoned.

Amanda thought long and hard. "Listen, I'll have him call you and give you the number. That way I won't get in trouble."

I never heard a word. Not one word. He became more and more famous. When people discovered that he'd lived across the street from me, they would press me for information. But I would clam up. "Oh, I barely knew him," I'd say. "We only spoke once or twice."

Almost fifteen years later, I was eating at my favorite watering hole. It's a wonderful café on Beverly Boulevard called the Kings Road Café, where they bake their own bread and the waiters are the cutest boys on earth. Well, who should I see walking up the street but Mr. Luke Perry. I screamed and ran up to greet him.

He was no longer a boy. He was a grown man. And he had aged beautifully—his once-cute features were now ruggedly handsome. I felt almost shy and, suddenly, all seemed to be forgiven.

He joined me and we sat and talked. He had two kids, a boy and a girl. He showed me pictures and they were adorable. He and his wife had split up, and he'd bought a farm somewhere in the South. He had fourteen calves and when he got fourteen more he would be able to live off that farm. His kids loved it. He said he might even give up show business and move there.

I completely forgot to be mad at him. I cannot tell you how it lightened my spirit to see him doing so well. Luke told me that I looked exactly the same. He told me that I had not changed at all. He gave me a big sweet kiss on the cheek, said goodbye, and off he went. I could not help but notice he still had a cute ass.

As he was walking away I yelled, "Hey! I finally got to see you naked!" referring to his nude scene on the television show *Oz*.

He turned around.

"Leslie, I had to take twelve steps butt-naked. I counted them. And do you know, on the second step I thought to myself, Leslie Jordan is going to love this!"

The Resilience of the Human Spirit

Om Namah Shivaya
The Great Redeeming Mantra

CHRISTINE CAVANAUGH is a brilliant actress who veered into voice work and enjoyed huge success. Christine has the look of a lost waif. She is all eyes, and she is real tiny, like me. She is blessed with this adorable, high-pitched voice that has become her claim to fame. She landed the voice of one of the main characters in the popular kids' cartoon *Rugrats* and also was the voice of Babe, the pig, in the Oscar-nominated film *Babe*.

The last time I saw Christine was when we both worked on a project with George Clooney. George was having a lot of success on *ER* and was trying his hand at producing. He had found an amazing script called "Nowhere Man," written by Ellen DeGeneres's brother and his writing partner at the time. George thought that "No-where Man" would make an excellent pilot, and his plan was to get a group of actors together, march us into the office of the president of NBC, and do a staged reading.

We were all invited up to George Clooney's big new house in one of the canyons above Studio City to rehearse. George shared the house with his beautiful French girlfriend at the time, Celine, and his pet pig, Max. After the rehearsal ended, Celine presented each of us with a blue Tiffany box. Inside was a sterling silver pen, beautifully engraved with the words *Thank you. Love, George.*

George Clooney is a real champion. He was born in the South (Lexington, Kentucky), where good manners are of the utmost importance.

As we were all leaving with our lovely presents, Christine asked me if I'd like to get a bite to eat or go have a drink. I told her that I couldn't. I had to return to the hospice where I volunteered, because one of my patients was about to make his "transition."

Project Nightlight was founded by a force of nature named Cassandra Christensen. In the early

1980s she was walking through the Miami airport and bumped into Mother Teresa. She physically bumped into the tiny nun and her entourage of sisters.

"Mother Teresa," Cassandra said, "I am a transition nurse who works with patients dying of cancer. You have been such an inspiration to me."

Mother Teresa looked up at Cassandra. "Do you work with AIDS?"

At that time, men and women were dropping like flies in the AIDS unit at Los Angeles County Hospital, which was the only AIDS unit in the county then. Because of the stigma attached to the disease, people were dying all alone. AIDS was seen as shameful and terrifying. Friends, family, even lovers were walking away, unable to deal with death on such a horrific level. Project Nightlight had a very simple mission statement: No one should die alone.

The volunteers started out wandering the halls of the AIDS unit with boxes of Popsicles. I am not sure whose idea that was, but it was genius. One of the side effects of the early medicines used to combat the virus was a dry mouth—and besides, what better reminder of an easier, simpler time than sharing a Popsicle with someone?

We would poke our heads in the doorways of complete strangers and ask, "Want a banana Popsicle?"

The patients were bordering on sensory deprivation because of their lack of human contact. Even the nurses were afraid to come too close. We would just sit, slurp our Popsicles, and let them talk. And boy, did they talk. We also found masseurs who were willing to come in and do back rubs while we all giggled and ate Popsicles.

The results were magical. The resiliency of the human spirit is astounding.

I had been assigned to Linn House, a hospice where gay men went to die after they had been given a prognosis of six months or less. In the 1980s and early 1990s, it was almost a daily occurrence.

I buried an entire phone directory.

That's what I did back then. I marked names out of my phone book and attended memorial services. And I would go on horrendous benders involving vodka and crystal methamphetamine. But who wouldn't? We were all too young to be burying our brothers and sisters. At least, that was the excuse I made back then. The excuses had changed over my many years of substance abuse, but that was the best one I'd come up with.

Now, in front of George Clooney's beautiful home, Christine spoke up. "I want to go with you."

"Trust me, Christine, you don't. It's not like the movies. It's not a bunch of friends sitting by the bedside whispering, 'Just let go . . . just let go.' It's horrible."

I explained what we had learned in our training about hospice care and the dying. The body is like an old clock, winding down. There are awful, awful noises. There really is a death rattle. And in this particular case, the patient had asked to not be resuscitated and was basically drowning as his lungs filled with fluid. It was almost too horrible to imagine.

But Christine had her own agenda. What that was, I was not sure, but she looked feverish and flushed, and very determined.

So off we went. Linn House sat in an old Hollywood neighborhood, on a lovely tree-lined street. The hospice was housed in a brand-new building that blended in with its lush surroundings, and inside there was soft music, art, lots of color, and nicely furnished rooms. It was a safe place to end a life's journey. It takes a certain kind of person to work with the dying, and Linn House had found the best of the best.

Christine and I were greeted with the news that Brian, my patient, was fighting hard. Brian was a fighter. He had the most difficult personality I had ever encountered. It seemed to be his mission in life to repel anyone who tried to love him. The volunteer coordinator at Project Nightlight had thought we'd make a good fit.

I had stuck with Brian through three other hospices he'd been booted out of for bad behavior. His crimes mostly involved mistreatment of the staff. He tended to think of the staff as his personal servants. He had also been kicked out of a few places for sexual misconduct. I did not want to know the particulars of those misdemeanors.

The one good thing that came out of the AIDS epidemic was that gay men began to seek new spiritual paths. So much of what we dealt with as kids seemed bogus when compared to what we faced now. We sought new paths to God.

Brian had embraced Hindu teachings. We would take little day trips to see his guru when

she was in town. This proved to be a little difficult, as Brian was incontinent and wheelchair
bound. But we made do with diapers and threw
his wheelchair in the back seat of my beat-up VW
Rabbit convertible.

Guru Ma Jaya is a magnificent creature who is
half Mother Teresa and half Bette Midler. In the
1970s she was a Jewish housewife in Brooklyn
when she had a spiritual awakening. She had a
vision of Christ in which He told her, "Teach all
ways, for all ways are my ways."

I loved Guru Ma Jaya. She was so seductive.
She was love incarnate. And boy, did she know
how to make an entrance! No wonder the gay
boys loved her. There was music, banging of
drums, dancing and singing disciples, throwing
of flower petals, and a lot of kissing and swirling
about until everything reached a crescendo. Then
Guru Ma Jaya would come out, dressed to the
nines. Her washboard abs peeked out from the
midriff of her brightly colored gold-trimmed sari,
she wore chic mule slippers and dangling gold
earrings, and her black hair was cut short, in punk
spikes. The red dot on her tanned forehead made
her a gorgeous creature not of this world.

Guru Ma Jaya would plant herself on the dais,

arrange her robes, and begin to talk. This was not what I was used to. There was no talk of hellfire and damnation. No hollering about lost sinners. No feverish altar call offering salvation from the Lake of Fire. Guru Ma Jaya offered a simple message of love. She stressed how the key to happiness on this plane of existence was to be of loving service to others. It was so personally cathartic.

When the AIDS epidemic hit, I had jumped into the trenches. We all did. Never let it be said that gays and lesbians do not take care of our own. And looking back on those days, I do not remember the sadness, I remember the love. Even though I was deep into my own disease of alcoholism, I was somewhat happy to be of loving service to others.

Brian was going to make his transition, and I had promised him that I would be there. I slowly led Christine down the hushed hallway to Brian's room. It was worse than I expected. Even though the nurses had lit candles around Brian's altar to Guru Ma Jaya and there was a tape of Hindu chants softly playing, he was in a tortured state. The skin of his face was stretched tight in a death mask. A horrible rattle was coming from his open mouth, and he would try repeatedly to sit forward so he could breathe. Up and down, like some macabre Halloween display. He was completely incoherent. He had been in a coma-like state for days.

I felt so helpless. Our hospice training had taught us that at this stage the only thing to do was make the patient as comfortable as possible. I set about arranging pillows under his neck to try and see if there was a position where he could breathe better.

I was startled from my busywork to see Christine standing at the foot of the bed. There were tears streaming down her face, and her mouth was open in a silent scream. I thought bringing her had been a huge mistake.

Then she spoke. "Crawl in bed with him and hold him."

"Christine, Brian was not a hugger. Trust me. Most of his waking energy was spent keeping people at bay. He kept everyone at arm's length."

"That is all the more reason to do it," she argued. "Crawl in bed with him and hold him. It's human nature to want to be held. If you don't do it, I will."

That seemed terribly inappropriate. I hesitated.

"My God," she said, "doesn't he have family? He's dying all alone."

I explained that there was a brother but they were estranged.

"You have to get in bed with him."

So I did. It was very awkward at first. I tried cradling him like a baby. I rubbed his arms and even touched his face. He seemed to relax a little. The death rattle almost stopped completely.

"Talk to him. Tell him it's okay to go. You have to give him permission."

How Christine knew all of this, I will never know. A lot of what she was saying had been brought up in our training. I began to talk softly in his ear. I tried to remember as much as I could about the teachings of Guru Ma Jaya. I tried humming along with the hypnotic Hindu chants.

"*Om Namah Shivaya.... Om Namah Shivaya.... Om Namah Shivaya....*"

But mainly, I just cooed. It was like talking to a baby. I'm not sure how long this went on, but when I looked up, Christine was gone.

And so was Brian.

Or so I thought.

Another horrible rattle came from his throat

and I knew that I could not take another minute in that room. Christine was waiting outside. I walked past her, down the hall, and out into the balmy Hollywood night. It's odd what you remember about times like this. Something about being close to death gives a heightened sense of the ordinary; I remember palm trees swaying in the moonlight and the exotic smell of the night-blooming jasmine. Christine followed but did not say a word.

We walked up to Santa Monica Boulevard to a bar I used to frequent. It was my home away from home. Hunter's was a real dive, what is known as a hustler bar. The patrons of Hunter's were primarily young, rough boys, thirty days out of Soledad prison. Most of them had chipped teeth, tattoos, dirty fingernails—and big monkeys on their backs. They were willing to do anything, and I do mean anything, for forty dollars.

Right up my alley. No high-priced hookers for this old whoremonger. I sat in Hunter's regularly for years, perched on a bar stool with a cocktail in one hand and my ATM card in the other.

My accountant once remarked, "You can always tell when Mr. Jordan is working—there's not a boy on the boulevard that does not have on brand-new tennis shoes."

Sometimes, when alcohol did not do the trick, I had to call the witch doctor. I would use the excuse when one of my patients died to go on a horrendous speed run. It was my dirty little secret. I was doing it years and years before it became popular. I had been using speed since all the way back in my college days. Back then it was in diet pill form. Black beauties, white crosses, speckled birds—"trucker speed," we called it. Rumor had it that a trucker with a handful of black beauties could drive from California to the tip of Maine in ten minutes.

Speed revs most people up and gives them a lot of energy and spunk. It makes them real talkative and lively. It works the opposite on me. It is the same principle as giving hyperactive children uppers. My whole body used to give a huge sigh of relief when I ingested amphetamines.

This was my routine, which I saw as a break from life. After barricading myself in my bedroom for six days (peeing in a jar because the speed made me too paranoid to go down the hall to the bathroom), mainly cleaning and watching tons of porno, I would venture out in the daylight to hire a hustler. It was never about sex. I seldom had sex. I would hire one of those unfortunate boys simply to come home and sit with me until I could fall asleep. I had become so isolated in my disease that I just needed human contact. And for some reason, those boys were beautiful to me. They were my damaged lower companions. Once I was sound asleep, they would rob me. It happened time after time after time. Sometimes I would forget and bring the same one back to rob me again!

But I had realized that the speed was going to kill me. Or make my teeth fall out, which was even worse. So I gave it up. I gave up speed cold turkey. It was pure hell. And then I began to drink with a vengeance.

Christine and I marched into Hunter's and took a seat at the bar, and without a word I began to drink. The last thing I remember is the bartender telling Christine that if she ordered drinks in her "Babe the Pig" voice, drinks were on the house.

I woke up the next morning sick as a dog and in a panic. I could not find the silver Tiffany pen

George Clooney had given me. I called Christine.

"I think you gave it to the Black Angel."

Apparently, as Christine and I sat at the bar, a black man came in and lurked behind us. Christine said he was dressed like a homeless person, with his pajamas sticking out. He stood behind us forever. Finally, I turned around and rudely asked him what he wanted.

"I've come from the Linn House," he said. "I thought y'all might want to know that Brian passed away right after y'all left. I'm in the room next to him. The nurses let me come over here to give y'all the news."

I became convinced he was an angel because I did not remember him residing in the room next to Brian, and no one from the hospice knew where we were. Had he followed us? Christine was almost certain I gave him my George Clooney pen as a token of my appreciation for bringing us the news. I was very distraught at this news. But it did make sense. I was a very giving drunk. I was always giving things away, mostly my money.

I ran over to Linn House. Brian's room was already stripped, awaiting another patient. So was the room next to Brian's. I asked the nurse about the Black Angel.

"Honey, that ain't no angel. Trust me. That was the Devil. We caught him hitting the crack pipe, right here in the Linn House! We tossed his butt out late last night."

Well, shit.

Many months later, I was perched on my bar stool at Hunter's and one of the bartenders walked over.

"I never really got a chance to thank you for the gift you gave me that night. I will always treasure that pen. I really will."

I sat there openmouthed. So I hadn't given my George Clooney pen to the Black Angel after all! Christine and I had run out of money, and I had used it as collateral to drink on. By the end of the evening, I had given the pen to the bartender for his kindness.

That was the last time I saw Christine. I miss her a lot. I think about her often, and hope she's well. I hope she has fond memories of our night with George Clooney, Brian, and the Black Angel. And most of all, I hope she treasures her pen.

Drugstore Cowboy

Never look back, darling; something might be *gaining* on you!

Tallulah Bankhead

SHORTLY AFTER yet another failed sitcom went off the air after only six torturous episodes, I was cast in a play that was being directed by my friend Renée Taylor. It was called *Wall of Water* and it starred a bunch of soap opera celebrities, and me. On opening night, Renée presented me with a lovely live gardenia bush. I was so touched. It already had a perfect bloom that gave off a scent that took me right back to the South of my childhood.

At the time, I was battling a teeny-tiny crystal methamphetamine addiction. I would go for days and days, unable to sleep. I was living in a craftsman-style bungalow in a rather seedy part of Hollywood. I had rented it because it was adorable and it had a banana tree in the front yard. But it was located two blocks south of Sunset Boulevard, where the female prostitutes hung out, and two blocks north of Santa Monica Boulevard, where the male prostitutes hung out. I had a front-porch swing where I could sit and observe everything. There was a steady stream of undesirables parading up and down my street every night. They were all heading either to the boulevards where they plied their trade or toward the crack houses that lay just blocks away from my cozy little home.

I sat on my porch thinking that I was above all that riffraff because I would *never* stoop to smoking crack. That was way too "ghetto" for me. I was too busy snorting crystal meth to calm my frayed nerves and having psychotic breakdowns. Yes, ma'am, slowly going bananas.

Since I never slept, I had to figure out all kinds of delightful projects to while away the time and keep me occupied. One night, at about 4 a.m., I decided to plant the gardenia bush that Renée Taylor had given me. As I dug in the dirt, I looked up and, to my surprise, I saw a cowboy strutting up the street. A real cowboy, with a belt buckle you could serve a turkey on, dirt-crusted boots, and an honest-to-goodness ten-gallon hat. He certainly wasn't coming from Oilcan Harry's—a gay cowboy bar over the hill in the San Fernando Valley where the boys look like cowboys, but when they open their mouths, fifty yards of purple chiffon flies out. No, ma'am. This was the real thing.

"Hey, man, you got a cigarette? I'm a little down on my luck."

Aren't they all?

He pulled off his hat, wiped his forehead— and I almost fainted. He was a redhead! I couldn't even speak. He was freckle-faced and had blue eyes that bored a hole through me. I put down my gardening tools, ran in the house without a word, and stole a cigarette out of the pack that Irma kept hidden in the kitchen drawer. She was wily like a fox, but I was always one step ahead of her.

"Thank you. Thank you very much."

My God, he sounded just like Elvis. I have always harbored a secret desire to have a boyfriend who looks and sounds like Elvis Presley. I almost had one once. His name was Don and he looked just like a young Elvis, at about the time he joined the military. But Don was from Cape Cod and quacked like a duck. This cowboy didn't look like Elvis but he sure sounded like him. I couldn't stop staring.

"You must be parched with all this traipsing around Hollywood at night. Would you like to come in for a glass of sweet iced tea?" I asked sweetly.

"You don't got no crystal meth, do ya?" he politely replied.

"Well, as a matter of fact, I do. Please, come this way."

And being a properly raised Southern hostess, I dusted the dirt off my knees, left my gardenia bush half-planted, and coyly led the way. He walked into my house and into my life and did not leave for four years. That gardenia bush sat in the yard unplanted until it turned brown and ugly—as did my life.

The cowboy was like a bad rash. I could not get rid of him—but Lord knows I didn't want to. I lived in desperate fear that he was going to leave me. He was a voracious drug user, had a horrible temper, and rarely even brushed his teeth or took a shower. He was a bigot, too, and even had a swastika tattooed on his hand! When I asked him what that was all about, he charmed me with a horrible story about his time in prison. After almost being raped by nine black men, he had gone to the only organization within the prison system that would help a good-looking white boy: the Aryan Brotherhood! The swastika was part of his initiation. It had been tattooed into his skin with ink from a pen, heat from a match, and an old rusty guitar string. He said he felt bad about it, but it saved his life while he was behind bars.

I could not bear to look at that tattoo. I told him when I could afford it I would pay to have it removed. But until then, I insisted he wear a Band-Aid. And off we'd go to industry parties, where I would make small talk with important Jewish people in the entertainment world standing beside my "boyfriend" with a hidden swastika tattoo.

It was a perilous existence, to say the least.

He was so dumb, he thought Farm Aid, Willie Nelson's yearly concert to help impoverished farmers, was in fact Willie Nelson's contribution to the fight against AIDS.

"You don't think about farmers getting AIDS, but they do. And when they get it, Willie's there for 'em. I got a lot of respect for him."

All I could say after that amazingly stupid observation was, "Please don't ever tell anybody what you just told me."

I have no idea why I am so attracted to the underbelly of life. I have always had an insatiable curiosity for anything that smacks of the tawdry. Perhaps it was because he was so good-looking and masculine. Or it could have been what was hiding in those tight Wrangler jeans. It was truly the eighth wonder of the world.

He was a big, strapping hunk of Southern manhood and I could not keep my eyes off him. Even the way he moved around the house fascinated me. It was terrifying, the hold he had over me. I would have done anything for him. What if we ended up on a cross-country crime spree? I was raised better than that!

Even with his mean streak and bullying ways, he could be as sweet and cuddly as a kitten when he wanted something, which was most of the time. Once he told me a very touching story. His daddy was a trucker who left the family of three boys when they were all little, but showed up again when they were in their early teens. He would take each boy on a long haul across the country during the summer. Since money was tight, instead of checking into a motel, they slept in the small bunk behind the driver's seat.

"Them times were the best times of my life," the cowboy said. "I'd curl up like a little ball right next to my daddy's big ol' beer belly. That's the only time I have felt safe in my whole miserable life."

At that moment I made up my mind that I would do anything within my power to give this boy a safe home. I would give him everything that life had denied him up to that point.

And then he asked me to buy him a dirt bike.

I often felt that there was not a homosexual bone in his body—he'd just learned to do whatever he needed to do to continue his drug habit. Deep down I knew that if I didn't make so much money working on those god-awful television shows to keep us high and buy him whatever he wanted, he wouldn't stay.

One time I bought him an Italian motorcycle that cost thousands and thousands of dollars. When the cowboy woke up it was parked in the driveway.

I handed him the keys. "Here. Now promise me you'll never leave me."

My accountant called and said, "A Ducati? Are you crazy?"

My life became a constant barter. Forget sex or even a little affection—I had to haggle just to keep him home and out of trouble. It was a major negotiation to make it through twenty-four hours without any drama. My self-esteem spiraled down to a little puddle of nothing. Addiction is not just about alcohol, drugs, gambling, sex, or whatever someone's particular vice is. We get addicted to people as well. I have never met an alcoholic or a junkie who did not also have issues of codependency. We give our power to other people. We let our happiness become dependent upon another person.

And that is hell on earth.

I have witnessed first hand the rage that crystal meth can induce. My four-year "relationship" was emotionally and physically abusive. And I was doing a lot of the abusing. I am four foot eleven and a wall of white blubbering flesh, but I learned to take care of myself. I am too much of a sissy to throw a punch, but I could certainly bitch-slap. And I learned to grab something like a kitchen chair or a beer bottle to hit back with when I got smacked.

Like a battered wife, I believed I was always the one at fault. I knew he had been up for days on speed. I knew his blood sugar was all messed up! So why did I push him to the point that he hit me? Why couldn't I control my temper?

Again and again the cops were called. It got so bad that Irma started doing her job with her pocketbook over her shoulder. She would vacuum, holding her purse. She'd be down on all fours, cleaning the toilet with her bag tucked under her arm. I told her it was okay to put it down, but she just pretended she didn't understand me. I never could figure out if she thought the cowboy might rob her or if she thought she might need to make a quick getaway.

That woman must have loved me more than my own mother did.

I walked into the house on New Year's Day and found him watching football. There was a case of beer in the fridge and he was drunk. I was livid. I had just spent an enormous amount of money sending him to rehab. I stomped into the kitchen and began banging pots and pans around to let him know of my dissatisfaction. He ambled in and stood watching me pitch my little fit.

"What's wrong, baby?"

At that point he leaned on the kitchen counter, tried to balance himself with his elbow, and a beautiful two-hundred-dollar ceramic fish plate crashed to the floor.

"See!" I screamed. *"See how you are!"*

I told him that gay men love their fish plates as much as straight men love their tools.

He snapped to attention. "Don't you dare touch my tools!"

Then he staggered back in to watch the game.

I decided right then and there I was going to fix his boat. I waited until he was almost asleep and tiptoed out into the garage. I stood for a long time staring at the big rolling tool chest I had bought him from Sears. He was so proud of it. He would spend hours and hours arranging and re-arranging the tools. That tool chest was off-limits! So I rolled it out by the swimming pool and slowly and methodically began to toss all his precious tools into the pool. Hell hath no fury like a little homo scorned.

I heard him come tearing out through the glass doors, but I didn't look at him.

"Look at this wrench, straight boy! Wheee!" *Plunk*. Right in the deep end.

"Leslie, I love you, but I will take . . . you . . . out."

Something about the tone of his voice made me turn around. He was swaying drunkenly, tears streaming down his face, one eye shut, and he was staring at me through the crosshairs of a crossbow.

I stared death right in the face and my first thought was, *Gee, he's crying. That is so sweet! He must really love me*. Was I a candidate for the rubber room or what?

We had rented a cabin up at Big Bear Lake that summer. When he got bored with his dirt bike he asked me to buy him a gun. "Are you crazy?" I asked. "You'll get high and shoot me."

Well, he caterwauled and carried on until he wore me down and I finally agreed to let him at least have a crossbow. I didn't really pay any attention to what it looked like. I just made him promise that he would not kill animals. He promised to use it only for target practice.

I would rather stare down the barrel of a gun than at that contraption. It was scary beyond belief. He had it cocked and ready to do harm. I screamed like a woman, and then he fired.

I ducked, but not quite in time. It caught the fleshy part of my arm. The cowboy took off running, and within seven minutes the place was swarming with cops. To this day, I do not know who called the police. But within minutes the cops had the cowboy on the ground in the front yard with their boots planted firmly on his neck. I got hysterical and cried that it was all a big mistake.

The police were very familiar with our "situation." They were appalled, and told me that brandishing a crossbow was a huge violation of his parole. And so they carted my beautiful, lost, redheaded cowboy back to prison.

He was eventually extradited back to Texas.

• • •

Many years later, my phone rang and I was informed by a recording that an inmate at a Texas penal institution was on the line. Would I accept the charges?

My heart started beating so hard I thought it would jump out of my chest. Against every cell in my body screaming to just hang up the phone, I accepted the call.

"Baby?"

Damn him! He still sounded just like Elvis.

"What do you want?"

"Hey, check this out, if you can come up with five grand, I got me a lawyer willing to reopen my case. I could get out! I could come back and live with you again in California. And I promise I'll be good this time. I promise, baby."

I could not believe what I was feeling. He still had a hold over me after all these years. I sat there with my eyes shut for a long time. I took a deep breath, and quickly cataloged all the things I had learned in recovery about self-love. I started talking slowly and deliberately because I was afraid I would run out of courage.

"Listen, believe it or not, I don't have the money. I really don't. And even if I did, I don't think I would give it to you. I have worked really hard to stay clean and sober for many years now. I've worked my ass off. I am more proud of my sobriety than of anything I have accomplished in my whole life. And even though, in some sick way, I will always love you, I am worth more than what you have to give. I wish you the best. I really do."

Click.

Robert Downey Jr.

There is always a moment in any kind of struggle when one feels in full bloom. Vivid. Alive. One might be blown to bits in such a moment and still be at peace.

Alice Walker

I ONCE spent a little time in the Big House with Robert Downey Jr. We were both locked up in the infamous Twin Towers in Los Angeles: section 152, pod A, cell 13. Robert was on top and I was on the bottom. In our bunk beds, of course.

After my disastrous relationship with the cowboy came to its violent end, I was on my own. I had lost or forgotten most of my coping skills, and I took a slide into oblivion. There is no one to blame. I was too far gone.

I will not bore you with my long drunkalogue, but I went to jail too many times to count during my final years of excess. How I managed to keep my career afloat is a mystery to me. Sometimes, late at night, I'll see a rerun of an old television show from that period in my life. I'm valiantly giving it my comedy best, but my eyes are dead.

Most of my arrests were for driving under the influence. Others were for several indiscretions I'd really rather not discuss right now. But I will say this: I was *not* shoplifting at Saks Fifth Avenue. And as for that tiny fracas involving someone urinating on the walls at a party I attended out in the Simi Valley, I happen to know for a fact the host of that party suffered from severe mental problems and was not to be believed. I mean, after all, would anyone in their right mind want to live out in the Simi Valley?

It is a huge source of shame that I used to drive drunk. When I was four years old, my father's mother, Aldine; his sister Dorothy; his sweet cousin Peggy; and his aunt Renee were hit head-on by a drunk driver on their way home from Christmas shopping. They were all killed instantly. Four lovely women in the prime of their lives, snatched away from us in an instant. The repercussions of that event reverberated through my family for years and years. This is not something that any drunk driver—including me, when I was one of them—ever thinks about. I drove drunk for years. Sometimes there were moments in the sober morning light when I worried I might kill a family of five and have to live with that the rest of my life, but such moments were few and far between.

All it took to quiet those thoughts was another drink.

Then I started getting caught. Time and time again I would see the lights flash in my rearview mirror.

Well, shit.

Sometimes I got in trouble and sometimes I didn't. A lot of times, I think they let me go because they recognized me from television. One time the cops asked me to do a very intricate sobriety test on the side of the highway. It involved putting my finger to my nose and then up my butt, all while reciting the Lord's Prayer and the Pledge of Allegiance backwards as I stood on one leg, or something like that. Well, I lost my balance and fell into the bushes.

I yelled, "How about best two out of three?"

They were not amused.

For reasons that made sense only to my alcohol-addled brain, I had moved to the San Fernando Valley, out in Van Nuys, about seven miles from where Christ lost his shoes. Poor Irma had to make three bus changes just to get to work. I was always caught two or three blocks from my house and hauled off to the Van Nuys jail. A sweet, older black woman ran the booking desk there. She would just slowly shake her head as I came walking in the door, handcuffed once again.

"Baby, baby, baby," she'd cluck. "Why can't you behave? You need to put a plug in the jug! Or we ain't gonna see you no more on them funny TV shows. They gonna send your drunk ass up the river."

And they did.

I was finally sentenced to thirty days for violation of my summary probation for my second DUI. No one in my family had ever been to jail for that long. I was so ashamed I told my mother I was at the Betty Ford Center, drying out.

When the judge first sentenced me, I almost swallowed my tongue. I was handcuffed, shackled, and put on one of those buses with cages to divide the seats. My lawyer stood on the street waving like I was leaving on a cruise. "Goodbye, Mr. Jordan! Make sure you ask for the homo tank! You'll never make it on the main line! Oh, and Mr. Jordan, take God with you!"

Take God with me? God and box of condoms!

When we got downtown, they handcuffed me to a little bench. There were four big redneck sheriffs down the hall, shooting the shit.

"Excuse me!" I called. "Excuse me!"

I was trying to put my voice in its lower register, but I was so nervous, it came out high and squeaky. I sounded like Richard Simmons encouraging a class of fat ladies, sweating to the oldies.

The sheriffs took one look at me and burst out laughing.

"What do you want, Little Bo Peep?" one of them asked, wiping tears from his eyes. "Did you lose your sheep?"

After all that, I certainly was not going to ask for the homo tank. I was too ashamed and intimidated. So they threw me right in the middle of the main line. Murderers, rapists, and thieves, oh my! It felt like I was back on the playground, where bullies rule. I assessed the situation and decided my chances of survival were slim to none. However, fate dealt me a winning card.

Years earlier, I had appeared in a movie called

Ski Patrol. I played Murray Tuttle, the head of the ski patrol. In the opening scene, I slip and fall in the snow, and a bulldog waddles over and farts in my face. The dog trainer had rigged some fishing line around the dog's face, and, when pulled, the line made it look like the dog was smiling. This gives you an idea of the caliber of humor. However, the movie also featured a then-unknown Mexican comedian named George Lopez. Well, George went on to have his own situation comedy and became a real hero to the Mexican people. I decided to use his "out of the barrio" success story to my advantage, since all the Mexicans on my cell block recognized me from *Ski Patrol.*

"Hey look, dude. It's the little dude from *Ski Patrol!* Ain't you the little dude from *Ski Patrol?* Hey, what's George Lopez like? Where my home-boy stay?"

I threw my arms up in the air like Rita Hayworth in *Gilda.*

"Gather 'round, boys! George Lopez stories for everyone!"

As I spun my yarns, I had those Mexican boys eating out of my hand. My mama didn't raise no fool. Nobody was going to bother me with my little posse hanging around. Those boys taught me all kinds of important things. Do you know that if you take a slice of moldy bread, ten packets of sugar, and rotten oranges and hang it all in a garbage sack behind the toilet, eventually it will turn into an alcoholic beverage? It is called perno and is quite tasty. And it packs a real wallop, too.

I have always suffered from a mild case of claustrophobia. Years ago, I used to get a panicked feeling in crowded discos. And I hate riding the subway in New York. I stand at armpit level and it is most unpleasant. On the seventeenth day of my incarceration, it hit me that I would not be leaving that small space for a really long time.

I freaked out and had a panic attack. I thought I was going to start screaming and clawing my face. When I would get really scared as a kid, I would pray. So that's what I did. I got down on my knees and prayed in my dark jail cell. How dramatic! I felt like Amanda Plummer in *Agnes of God*.

Dear God,
  If you are out there, which I highly doubt,
  I guess you know my heart and you know that

I am a nonbeliever. But you might remember me. I was a young Royal Ambassador for Christ at the Central Baptist Church in Chattanooga, Tennessee. Does that ring a bell? I was quite the little devotee. Um, I've taken a little detour here. I'm in the LA County lockup. Please get me out of this horrible jail cell and I will never drink or do drugs again. I'll dedicate my life to helping others stay clean and sober, I promise. Amen.

Well, at that moment, the turnkey appeared outside my cell.

"Mr. Jordan, we have good news and bad news. The good news is that we have Robert Downey Jr. downstairs and we have nowhere to put him, so he's in, and you're out. The bad news is that because you came in on a drunk driving charge we can't let you go until the bars close. You ain't leaving here till two a.m. So you and Mr. Downey will be sharing a cell in the holding tank."

Well, hallelujah! Robert Downey Jr.! I forgot all about my claustrophobia. I wanted to go over and thank him, but I wasn't sure it was appropri-

ate. He didn't look very chipper or like he was
feeling chatty, so I left him alone. But I sure did
enjoy the few hours we spent together.

Almost four years later, I got a job on *Ally McBeal*.
I called my mother with the script in hand to find
out which actor played what part, since I never
watch television. All my scenes were with a character named Larry Paul.

Mother knew the show well. "That character
is played by Robert Downey Jr."

Dead silence.

"Leslie, are you there?"

"Yes, ma'am. I was once in jail with Robert
Downey Jr."

"Well, I wouldn't tell anybody," Mother said.

"I don't plan on announcing it to the cast. I
just wonder if he'll remember me. I hope it isn't
awkward."

"Well, just be sweet. And be yourself. I'm sure
it will all work out."

I love my mother.

She is always hoping for the best.

The first day on the set, the assistant director
took me into the makeup trailer. It was the first
time I had seen makeup being applied with an

airbrush. It was the latest thing. It gives a very smooth, matte finish that is perfect for harsh television lighting. Calista Flockhart was leaned back in the chair, having her face hosed. I was fascinated.

The assistant director said, "Leslie, have you met Robert?"

I turned around and there he was.

He took one look at me and asked, "Have we met?"

What was I supposed to say? I just shook his hand and mumbled, "I don't think so. Pleased to meet you."

Later on in the day, he came up to me. "I feel like we've met."

I leaned in and whispered, "We were in jail together. We didn't really meet, but we were in the same holding tank. Actually, I got out because of you. There wasn't enough room."

He studied me intently. "You wrote me that letter."

I had completely forgotten. There was this poor boy in our cell block who was HIV-positive. Besides the fact that it was nearly impossible for him to get his medication, the other prisoners treated him like a pariah. No one would go near him. He was such a sad little creature that I be-friended him. The first time I sat down to eat with him, tears welled up in his eyes. I was worried about who was going to watch after him when I left, so I wrote to Robert Downey Jr., asking him to please be kind to my new friend. I thought that maybe the other prisoners would leave him alone if someone like Robert Downey Jr. took an interest.

I wasn't sure whether he ever got my letter or not. But I gave it a try.

Robert looked me right in the eye. "That let-ter really meant a lot to me."

We worked together for two days but had very little time to talk. I kept looking for an op-portunity, but it never happened.

I'm not sure who or what ever heard me, but I kept the promise I made in my prayer the night I spent in jail with Robert Downey Jr.

That was December 11, 1997.

My Ministry

No one could tell me where my soul might be.
I searched for God, but God eluded me.
I sought my brother out, and found all three.
Ernest Crosby, "The Search"

I WAS greeting people after a performance of my one-man show *Like a Dog on Linoleum* in Atlanta, Georgia, when this woman took my hands and, with tears in her eyes, told me I had a ministry.

Trying to lighten the moment, I laughed and said, "Oh, no, honey. Tammy Faye Bakker has a ministry, not me!"

But she persisted. "But you do, Mr. Jordan. The story you told tonight of your journey into acceptance is so important. It makes so much more sense than anything I've ever been taught or led to believe about God."

This woman had a gay son and had wrestled with her deeply devout belief that he was going to burn in hell. I, too, have struggled with that feeling. I have wrestled with the Devil for half my life. I have been baptized fourteen times! It never did take. The preacher would holler, "Come forward, lost sinner! Walk down the aisle and be saved!" And I would run down the aisle in sheer terror.

Sometimes the preacher would say, "Son, you came forward last week and the week before that, *and* you walked the aisle twice during the revival meeting. You are already saved! Please, remain seated!"

But I couldn't help it. I certainly did not feel saved. I knew I was a little homo, and I was scared to death of that Lake of Fire. I was a very imaginative kid and I could just picture Beelzebub reigning supreme over a bunch of sinners burning in eternal hellfire. My fear stayed with me well into adulthood. I've spent half my life worried about going to hell.

I remember that the first time I took Ecstasy it all came to a head. For anyone not in the know, Ecstasy is a designer drug used to induce a wonderfully euphoric feeling, but it can turn on you like a mother-in-law. It can also cause hallucinatory sights and sounds; you don't know what the hell is going on. I used to love that feeling. Back then I would swallow anything you handed me.

My little posse and I were tripping our brains out on Ecstasy and we decided to go to the Probe, which was a leather bar. It was hosting a "black party," an event where leather queens trot out all their finery. I was fresh off the turnip truck—still wearing khaki pants, button-down oxford cloth shirts, and penny loafers with no socks—and I stuck out like a rat turd on rice.

As we walked into the Probe, we looked down upon an enormous dance floor. There were hundreds and hundreds of beautiful gay men in all kinds of decadent attire and in all kinds of drug-induced stupors, dancing and waving their arms in the air. I was transfixed. I watched, deeply fascinated, when all of a sudden, every light on the dance floor turned red, and the whole club seemed to pulse with a trippy red glow.

And I saw it. I saw the Lake of Fire. I saw it as plain as the nose on my face, and it was a sea of burning cocksuckers.

It scared the shit out of me. Much to the dismay of my friends, I started screaming and took off all the way up Highland Avenue. I turned left on Sunset Boulevard and kept going. The sun came up the next morning and I was still running from the Devil. I made it almost to the Pacific Ocean.

On the long walk home, I came to my senses. I decided I would not waste another minute of my precious time on earth worrying about the Lake of Fire.

My mother was told by a nosy neighbor that I was sneaking out to gay bars at age seventeen, and she sent me to a Christian therapist. There is no one to bless and no one to blame for this. My mother had my best interests at heart. She loved me deeply, and it tears me apart when I think what she must have gone through. She had buried my daddy, the love of her life, and was left with the enormous responsibility of raising his troubled firstborn son. She made the best possible decision given the circumstances.

I unburdened my soul to that Christian therapist. After hearing my story, he told me, and I quote, "When you have these unchristian thoughts, these sexual thoughts about someone of the same sex, it is the voice of the Prince of Darkness that you are hearing."

What the fuck? Was this the Dark Ages? Do you know when people began depicting Satan as a red man with horns in Bible stories and pictures? Medieval England, that's when.

I remember thinking, *Well, the Prince of Darkness sure has a loud voice.*

I was consumed with sexual thoughts. And so is every other red-blooded seventeen-year-old boy, whether he is heterosexual or homosexual. My goodness gracious, that's why boys that age wear their shirts untucked, to cover their erections! Their hormones are running amok, and it is perfectly natural. But my thoughts weren't about girls, and I thought I was the only dirty little queer on the face of this earth. And that was a very scary place to be, especially when I knew deep within my heart that I was born that way. There was no choice.

I am and always will be attracted to people of my own gender. Why? I don't know. It's a mystery to me. But I do know that I had no more choice in the matter than I did about how the color of my skin was determined. And it is just as defining. I am flatlined on the homo side of the Kinsey scale. And with all due respect to Mr. Kinsey and the bisexual community, I firmly believe that we are all born predominately heterosexual or homosexual. What you do with it after that is up to you.

A certain evangelist can rail till the cows come home about his "dark side" after getting caught doing drugs and having sex with another man for three years. He can swear that he is not gay. I have news for him: Most straight men, if they are looking for an extramarital affair, do not seek out other men on the Internet for sex. And if they do, they certainly don't continue the relationship for years and years. He is a homosexual. His God made him that way.

If he wants to consider it his cross to bear, then so be it. Let him go through life fighting all those "dark urges." Let him squeeze his eyes shut, think about that handsome new man in his congregation butt-naked, and make love to his poor wife. But he will be a homosexual till the day he dies. There is nothing sadder than a man at war with his own nature.

I would never in a million years try to talk intelligently and passionately about the African-American experience, the Latino experience, or what it was like to grow up Asian. I know nothing about those things. But I do know what it means to be gay. I have had over fifty years' experience. Trust me, I've done my research.

I was once invited to a church service where Tammy Faye Bakker was preaching and the legendary Dottie Rambo, the most prolific writer of gospel music in the history of that genre, was performing. I had heard that the service was being held in a church in Hollywood that was known for ministering to gays and lesbians who wanted to "change their sinful ways."

I invited thirty of my sinful friends—all gay, all men, all recovering Southern Baptists—and off we went to see the show. We planted ourselves in the front pew. The preacher took the stage, and he was by far the most effeminate man I had ever beheld. Next to him, I looked like a Hell's Angel. He had a tanning booth tan and frosted hair, and he wore skintight black clothes that were more fitting for a disco than for a church service.

He was a real screamer!

His story was that he used to be gay but now, through the miraculous power of Jesus Christ, he wasn't. He said "my wife" eleven times within the first five minutes, just to make sure we all got it. He cried buckets about how honored he was to have Tammy Faye Bakker and Dottie Rambo in his humble church. He paraded out his sweet, clueless little wife and they sang a duet. She was a lovely soprano, and he was a very high tenor.

Then Dottie Rambo cut loose and brought the house down. She was not in good health, so they'd had to wheel her out in a wheelchair, but boy, there was nothing wrong with that woman's lungs. The preacher got back up, cried some more, and then out trotted Tammy Faye Bakker.

This was all a few years before Tammy Faye passed away. I once had the honor of opening for her at the Annenberg Theater in Palm Springs, California, when she was touring with her secular one-woman show. As a joke, I came out in full drag. I had on great big fake eyelashes in homage to her. Tammy Faye and I were the same height in our high heels. We sang a lovely unrehearsed version of "Singin' in the Rain."

The place went ape shit.

There was not a more sincere, loving person on the face of this earth than Tammy Faye Bakker. When I first met her, I was a little dubious about how naïve she seemed. I thought maybe that was her sneaky way of letting the world know she had no idea that her first husband, Jim, was bilking the congregation. But the more time I spent around her, the more I realized how genuine she was. She had the trusting nature of a child, and a heart of gold.

I thought she had been duped, along with Dottie Rambo, to appear at this Hollywood church, because when Tammy Faye began to preach, it was not what anyone expected.

"I am so angry at the Christian church in America today," she began. "I do not see the teachings of Jesus Christ anywhere. Jesus taught us not to judge. Jesus lay with the lepers, for goodness sakes! You will not find anywhere in the teachings of Jesus the mention of homosexuality. He teaches about thousands of things but never once is homosexuality mentioned."

I was riveted to her every word. *This,* I thought, *is what a Christian should sound like.* She talked of love and tolerance. She talked about how so many Christians judged her when her world fell apart, people who did not even know her. She talked about the reality show she had appeared in on national television with porn stars and all kinds of supposed riffraff. She had embraced those people and tried not to judge them. She tried to live by example. She got over ten thousand e-mails from all over the country thanking her for showing the world how a Christian woman really should act.

She won us over. You would have thought we were at a tent revival meeting in the Deep South the way we gay boys whooped and hollered. Several of my friends even went forward during the altar call to be saved. Tammy Faye Bakker became one of our biggest cheerleaders, headlining at Gay Pride events. She walked the walk and talked the talk.

Of course, later on we heard that the sissy preacher had resigned amid allegations that he had coerced one or more male congregants into having sex.

I read a quote recently in a magazine that described two types of gay people in America: the fabulous and the fearful. Those of us who live in the big cities surrounded by our tribe are the fabulous ones. But we forget that there are still gay men and women out in our hinterlands who are afraid, especially our gay youth. They are deathly afraid of someone finding out. They are afraid of what might happen.

Gay, lesbian, transgender, and bisexual youth are three times more likely than their straight counterparts to commit suicide.

I am very involved in an organization called the Trevor Project. It is a national hotline for suicidal gay, lesbian, transgender, bisexual, and questioning youth. When they plugged in a few years ago, they got fifteen thousand calls within the first few months.

Most of those calls came from the Bible Belt. That breaks my heart. I think telling a child about Satan and the Lake of Fire is spiritual abuse—borderline child abuse. If people choose to believe in the Devil, then so be it. But if they raise their children to fear God, then I think there is something radically wrong with their parenting skills. The idea of God, if one chooses to believe in God, should be a safe haven, a place for a child to go for comfort in times of trial and tribulation.

I do not, for one minute, believe that somewhere out there is a fallen angel named Lucifer, who is tending a lake of fire for sinners. I find the story of Jonah living in the belly of a whale very suspicious, and I definitely do not believe that Lot's wife looked back and turned into a pillar of salt.

That is impossible!

Those were fables passed down from generation to generation by men who lived out in the sand. I see the Bible as a wonderful teaching tool filled with amazing, allegorical stories. But do I think that the Bible is the definitive word of God, as I was so lovingly raised to believe? No more so than I believe that the Torah, the Koran, the teachings of the Buddha, the teachings of Muhammad, or the teachings of all the other great spiritual leaders throughout time are the definitive word of God.

There are many paths to God.

I read somewhere that religion is for people who are afraid of going to hell, and spirituality is for people who have already been there. I like that. It makes sense to me. And that is what I am striving for, a spiritual path that makes sense to me.

The arrogance and the stupidity of one group believing that their book is the only book really gripes my ass. As Guru Ma Jaya says, "When they say their way is the only way, run the other way!"

I am not as interested in the separation of church and state as I am in the separation of church and hate. In a wonderful article in the *San Francisco Chronicle,* Deepak Chopra said; "You'd think that someone would stand up and ask a simple question: Who are we to condemn gays if Christ didn't? In fact, who are we to condemn any sinner, since Christ didn't? . . . The reversal of Christianity from a religion of love to a religion of hate is the greatest religious tragedy of our time."

Actually, the book of Leviticus lists all kinds of things that are punishable by death—from eating shellfish to adultery to rebelling against your parents to screwing your wife while she's having her period. The handling of pigskin is listed as a big no-no. Whoops! There goes football.

I mean, did Jesus not clearly say to turn the other cheek?

Here is a quote from *USA Today*: "Galileo was persecuted for revealing what we now know to be truth regarding Earth's place in the solar system. Today, the issue is homosexuality, and the persecution is not of one man but of millions. Will Christian leaders once again be on the wrong side of history?"

It took the Catholic Church 376 years to admit that the earth did indeed revolve around the Sun.

And it is happening again.

Are we in the midst of a culture war? You bet your sweet ass we are. We are in the throes of the greatest civil rights movement since the 1960s. And I am thrilled to be a part of it. We will prevail—and it is going to happen in my lifetime.

This I know.

The Soul Has No Gender

Out beyond ideas of wrongdoing and rightdoing, there is a field. I'll meet you there.

Rumi, thirteenth-century Persian mystic

WHEN I was growing up as a Baptist, I had a friend with whom I shared a very shameful secret. It was not *the* secret, although we harbored that, too. Our secret was so shameful that I swore I would go to my grave without telling anyone. When we were little boys and no one was home, my friend and I would dress up in my mother's clothes, stand before the mirror with a hairbrush as a microphone, and pretend we were Diana Ross and the Supremes. We had no idea what a drag queen was. We just loved pretending we were Diana Ross and the Supremes.

I took my mother's bathrobe and fashioned myself a lovely gown. I would put the robe on backwards, let it fall off my shoulders, and then cinch it at the waist. Then my friend and I would put on our pretend high heels and prance around on our toes. And it's probably not widely known, but during those daring days, I accidentally invented the Farrah Fawcett shag, way before anyone had even heard of Miss Fawcett. I would sneak into my mother's closet, pull out her wig, and try it on. It always looked a little boring, so one day, in a fit of inspiration, I flipped the wig completely upside down. Voilà! It looked like shit from the back, but I was good to go in the front.

I was always, always Diana Ross. "Are you going to be the backup girl?" I'd ask my friend. "Then back the fuck up!"

My little friend and I would bring down the house with our stunning renditions of all the Supremes' songs. I love that the two little queers in our great big church found each other. And do you know, we were best friends all the way through high school, but never once did we mention the things we did when we were little boys.

Eventually my friend took a much different path. He married a beautiful girl who was the daughter of a doctor. They were married for a couple of years before I heard through the grapevine that they had gotten divorced. And then my friend just disappeared.

Twenty years later, I was walking down the street in West Hollywood, where there are queers hanging from the trees, and there he was. I couldn't believe it.

I asked, "Where on earth have you been?"

"Oh, honey," he said, "I've been having a Homo Hoedown!"

He was the very first person I knew to be diagnosed with the AIDS virus. This was in the early 1980s, and a few years before I began my work with Project Nightlight. Back then, AIDS was terrifying. If you visited someone in the hospital, you had to wear a complete space suit, mask and all.

But for some reason, with my friend, I was fearless. I'd like to think that my colossal bravery was because of my enormous heart and my love for all mankind, but I think it may have actually had more to do with the amount of crystal meth I was snorting. I read once something about Hitler giving his troops amphetamines, because it gave the troops a feeling of invincibility and made them too paranoid not to fight.

I would sit with my friend night after night, high as a kite. All my friends would exclaim, "Leslie, I don't know how you do it!"

What else did I have to do? Go home and watch porno movies? At that point, my life had shrunk to almost nothing. Plus, it became my job to dole out his medicine. Now *that* was a lot of fun!

"Here you go, sweet baby, one for you and two for me. . . ."

I'd even let him smoke cigarettes. He was on oxygen! As we both lit our Virginia Slims, I'd say, "Be careful of that tank, girl. You'll blow us to kingdom come!"

We would sit together, smoking, giggling, and talking up a storm. We used these endless nights to catch up. We laughed and laughed about our diva days pretending we were Diana Ross and the Supremes. Sometimes on his good days we'd get up and act it all out again. We would even make beautiful gowns out of hospital robes. We talked about everything under the sun except his illness. I instinctively knew that was off-limits. Then one day out of the blue he went crazy on me.

I didn't know back then what we know

now—that sometimes AIDS patients suffer from dementia. I just thought he'd gone bonkers. He began to rattle on incessantly. He would spew forth babble with absolutely no segue. But, you know, I was tweaking so hard on speed a lot of it actually made sense!

"Mmm-hmm, yeah, I'm with you on that one, girl."

One night, at about 5 a.m., he had finally quieted down, bless his heart. I was staring out the window, smoking my last cigarette, and waiting for those goddamn birds to start chirping. All of a sudden, I heard a tiny voice.

"Leslie . . . do you think I'm being punished?"

I had a minor panic attack. It didn't help that I was out of my mind from the drugs. At the time, the preachers in the Deep South were all saying the same thing, that AIDS was God's punishment for homosexuality. Ironically, if you had been raised as I had, it made a lot of sense. It was a tumultuous time for gay men who had been raised in the church.

My friend would not let up. In his dementia it became his mantra.

"Do you think I'm being punished? Do you think I'm being punished?"

He would repeat this over and over again, like a parrot. And no matter how many times I tried reasoning with him, he would act as if he didn't even hear me.

"Do you think I'm being punished? Do you think I'm being punished?"

Three days before he died, he sat up in bed and he was as lucid as I had ever seen him.

"Leslie, the most amazing thing has happened. I prayed last night, and God spoke to me."

You must understand that in the Baptist church we heard that stuff all the time. The preacher was always shouting about speaking to God: "And then He spoke to me! Whoopee! We got the Devil on the run!"

So when my friend told me that God had spoken to him, I walked over to where my stash was, chopped out a line of crystal, and snorted it. "Well, isn't that something? That just tickles me pink. I can't wait to hear what He said."

It all went over the top of my poor, drug-addled head.

By this time, my friend was nothing more than a little burned-up french fry, but he took my hand with what seemed like superhuman strength, and pulled me down on the bed beside him. He was so weak he could barely talk above a whisper.

"Leslie, it's important that you listen, because I heard Him. I heard the voice of God. And it is so simple. See, first of all . . . the soul has no gender. So when it is all said and done, it is not about whom one loved that is important. What is important is the quality of that love. We are on this earth for one reason and one reason only. And that is to give quality love on a daily basis."

I sat holding his hand for a long time.

He died three days later in complete peace.

Many, many years later, when I finally sobered up, those words began to resonate. The whole recovery movement is based upon the idea that true recovery from any addiction springs from a spiritual awakening. It really is one day at a time. We are granted a daily reprieve from our addiction, based upon our spiritual maintenance. I think it was a stroke of genius to add the words "God as we understood him" when the twelve steps were written. Otherwise I would have been in trouble, and so would lots of other spiritually damaged people trying to get clean and sober. I never would have been able to kick drugs and alcohol if I had been told to lean on the stern and punishing God of my childhood.

Even after having what many would consider a true religious experience at the bedside of my friend who was dying of AIDS and praying on my knees in a jail cell, I still have doubts. Did my friend really hear the voice of God or did he hear what he needed to hear, in order to die in peace? Did god have anything to do with me getting out of jail, or was it just synchronicity? I don't know. I have quit trying to figure it out. I just know that I am like a dog with a bone. I chew on things.

The best I can do is seek, on a daily basis. My heart is open. And I am of the opinion that those of us who seek are actually in a much better position when bad things happen than those who have blindly accepted a belief that was handed to them.

I think the most important spiritual axiom of the last two millennia is: Shit happens!

And it does. Really bad things happen to really good people and really good things happen to really bad people. Where is God in that? When I read about thirty-three people being gunned down on a college campus and one of them a nineteen-year-old girl who had dedicated her life to spreading the wonderful news of Jesus Christ, I think, *Where is God in that?* "It was God's will" is a huge cop-out. And "It is not up to us to question God's will" is pretty lame, too.

Was it God's will that thousands of good, churchgoing people were left homeless and destitute in the wake of Hurricane Katrina? Is it God's will when innocent children are molested or murdered? And people suffering from cancer, is that God's will, too?

Shit happens and I don't think God has anything to do with it.

I love the idea of having a God that does not do anything for me or to me, but only shines *through* me. I love the idea of God as a light, a beautiful, all-encompassing, nonpunishing, healing light of love. I love the idea of having a God that does not write books. *That* never made any sense to me anyway. He wrote several best sellers—why did He stop? What has He been doing all these *thousands* of years? Did He get writer's block? And which of the books that He wrote so long ago does He count as His Truth? The Bible? The Torah? The Koran? And don't even get me started on the Book of Mormon.

What's up with all that?

All religions are man-made, and all books about religion are written by man (or woman).

When I first heard those words from someone sharing in my recovery group, I thought that was the scariest thing I had ever heard. I waited for lightning to strike the building. I felt bereft and rudderless. But the more I allowed these thoughts to creep into my consciousness and the more I incorporated these ideas into my belief system, the more things began to make sense.

And thus began my journey.

It was then and only then that I was able to find a spiritual path that worked for me. If a person has found an amazing and comforting spiritual path within an organized religion, that is wonderful. Millions and millions of people have. Good for them. But it didn't happen for me. I garner what I can from all spiritual writings and teachings, and what doesn't work for me, I leave behind. I don't have to leave logic and reason at the door to have faith.

My spiritual path is intensely personal. I have slowly learned to follow my own spiritual path. It really is about the journey. I feel it is up to me to keep the channel open so the light can shine through. I was taught early in my recovery that there are three things that keep us from the sunlight of our spirit: our fears, our resentments, and our sexual misconduct. I learned to write on a daily basis about all of these things. When the scary monsters under the bed begin their low moan, I write in my journal. It slows my mind down to the speed of a pen, which helps me gain clarity. I read my writings out loud to someone whom I trust, usually my spiritual advisor. Then we decide what path I'll take and whether there are amends to be made.

I write to keep the conduit open so the light can shine through me.

And oddly enough, it is in all this writing, all this seeking, that I have found my faith and acceptance. I have found so many wonderful, wonderful things. I found that happiness is a habit. Happiness is a choice. And happiness is something you have to really work hard at. I found that love is not a noun. Love is a verb. And it is in the action of offering loving service to others that we receive our self-love. I have found that the greatest healing force is laughter, and I have been blessed to have the gift, as my daddy told me, of being able to make people laugh.

I treasure that gift.

Maybe I do have a ministry. I don't know. I try to live a life of attraction, not promotion. But I often think about the young gay man or woman, out in the Bible Belt, or wherever, perhaps lying in bed, staring at the ceiling, awash in feelings of shame, fear, guilt, and self-loathing. I think about that person wondering, as I wondered, if there is a God who loves queers.

It breaks my heart.

There is so much work to be done. I want that young gay man or woman to know what I have learned on my journey. It is up to me to pass it on. My crazy, convoluted tale, for what it's worth. My trip down the pink carpet.

Because these are my stories.

These are my songs.

Acknowledgments

First and foremost, I must acknowledge that this book would have never happened had my dear friend Michael Broussard not pestered me relentlessly to write down some of my best dinner party stories so he could pitch a book idea. He, along with my dream team at Simon Spotlight Entertainment—Jen Bergstrom; Jen Robinson; Michael Nagin; Martha Schwartz; Jennifer Weidman; and my amazing editor, Ursula Cary—worked tirelessly to bring it all to fruition.

I want to thank Dave Morgan and his team at Reaction Marketing along with my dear, long-time manager, Billy Miller, for arranging the original thirty-city tour to promote the book.

Thanks also to my twin sisters, Janet and Cricket Jordan, for working so hard to find great pictures to spice things up!

Big kisses to the fabulous photographer Jim Cox for allowing me to use that great picture of me on a park bench gazing longingly at my handsome friend Brannon Purvis on the grounds of the Parker Hotel in Palm Springs.

And last, but certainly not least, I would like to thank my spiritual adviser, Don Norman, for his constant and astute advice on "trudging the road of happy destiny."

About the Author

LESLIE JORDAN hails from Chattanooga, Tennessee. Standing at just four feet eleven inches, he has become an instantly recognizable face in film and television. He is best known for his role as Beverley Leslie in the hit series *Will & Grace*, for which he won an Emmy in 2006. He lives in Los Angeles.